TOWNS, TRAILS & SPECIAL TIMES

The Marlboro Country Cookbook

In its towns, along its trails, or on its special days,
the food somehow tastes different here.

It might be the recipes. Mostly memorized.
With measures done by hand and eye.

It could be the ingredients. Sometimes fiery, sometimes bold.
Always plain and simple.

Part of it, is the morning light coming through a cafe's window.
The scent of sourdough, mesquite and coffee out on the range.
And the sound of company coming, same time every year.

Marlboro Country.
Somehow, things taste different here.

Cafes

HOT CINNAMON BUNS

1	Tbsp. active dry yeast	⅓	cup sugar
½	cup lukewarm water	2	tsp. chili powder,
¾	cup lukewarm milk		optional
½	cup sugar	1	tsp. each, ground
½	cup soft butter or		cinnamon and
	margarine		coriander
1½	tsp. salt	¼	tsp. each, ground
2	eggs		cloves, allspice
4 to 5	cups all-purpose flour		and cardamom
¼	cup soft butter or	1	cup chopped semi-
	margarine		sweet chocolate pieces

Dissolve yeast in warm water in large mixing bowl. Add milk, ½ cup sugar, ½ cup butter, salt, eggs and

3 cups flour; beat until smooth. Beat in additional flour until a soft dough is formed.

Turn dough out onto a floured surface; knead until smooth and elastic, about 5 minutes.

Place in a buttered bowl; turning dough to

Use string to cut log. Knives give you crushed ends.

butter top. Cover and let rise in a warm place until doubled, about 1½ hours. Punch down; cover and let rest 5 minutes.

Turn out onto a lightly floured surface; roll into a 16x18-inch rectangle. Spread with ¼ cup softened butter.

Combine ⅓ cup sugar and spices; sprinkle over dough. Sprinkle chocolate pieces over sugar.

Roll up tightly starting at the 16-inch side. Pinch end to seal. Cut into 8 slices (see picture). Place in a greased 13x9-inch baking pan.

Let rise until double, about 40 minutes. Bake in a 375° oven for 25 to 30 minutes. While warm, spoon over Vanilla Glaze.

MAKES 8 BUNS.

Vanilla Glaze: *Mix together until smooth: 2 cups confectioners' sugar, ¼ cup milk and 1 tsp. vanilla.*

CORNMEAL WAFFLES

1¼ cups all-purpose flour
½ cup cornmeal
2 Tbsp. sugar
2 tsp. baking powder
½ tsp. salt
3 eggs, separated
1¾ cups milk or buttermilk
4 Tbsp. melted butter
   or margarine
Vegetable oil
1 cup chopped pine nuts
   or pecans

Combine flour, cornmeal, sugar, baking powder and salt in a mixing bowl. Beat egg yolks with milk; beat in flour mixture and melted butter. Beat egg whites until stiff peaks form; fold in a small amount of cornmeal batter, then fold whites into remaining batter. Heat waffle iron, brushing with oil, if needed. Pour batter onto hot waffle maker, sprinkle with chopped nuts; close top and bake until steam stops and waffles are golden brown and crisp, about 5 minutes. Serve immediately.

MAKES 4 OR 5 SERVINGS.

FRUIT JUICE SYRUP

2 cups grape, cranberry or
   apple juice
2 Tbsp. lemon juice
2 tsp. liquid pectin
3 cups sugar

Combine fruit juice, lemon juice and pectin in a 2½ to 3-quart saucepan; mix well. Place over high heat and bring to a boil.

Add sugar, stirring to melt sugar. Bring to a full boil and boil 3 minutes. Cool and pour into jars. Refrigerate. Will keep in refrigerator for 3 weeks.

MAKES ABOUT 3½ CUPS.

NO COOK BERRY TOPPING

2 pints fresh strawberries
4 cups sugar
2 Tbsp. lemon juice
⅓ cup liquid pectin

Wash and dry berries, removing stems. Mash or crush fruit, about 2½ cups, and put into a large bowl.

Stir sugar into fruit, add lemon juice; let stand for 10 minutes. Add pectin and stir constantly for 3 minutes. Pour into clean freezer containers.

Let stand for 24 hours. Refrigerate or freeze for future use. Will keep in refrigerator for 3 weeks.

MAKES ABOUT 5 CUPS.

Sweet Grain Bread

1 cup milk	¼ cup lukewarm water
⅓ cup maple syrup	2 cups all-purpose flour
2 Tbsp. butter or margarine	⅓ cup millet or sesame seeds
1 Tbsp. molasses	¼ cup bran flakes
1½ tsp. salt	1½ to 2 cups whole wheat flour
1 package active dry yeast	

Heat milk to boiling; remove from heat and add syrup, butter, molasses and salt.

Soften yeast in lukewarm water in mixing bowl; let stand until bubbly. Add first mixture. Beat in all-purpose flour, millet and bran. Stir in 1 cup whole wheat flour.

Turn onto a lightly floured surface. Knead until smooth and elastic, about 5 minutes, adding whole wheat flour as needed. Butter a large bowl; place dough in it, turning to butter top. Cover and let rise until double, about 1½ hours. Punch down.

Shape into 1 loaf; place in a greased 8½-inch loaf pan. Let rise until double, about 45 minutes. Bake in a 350° oven for 40 minutes.

MAKES 1 LOAF.

Montana Omelet

6 large eggs	¼ cup finely chopped onion
½ cup sour cream or half-and-half	1 cup chopped, cooked potatoes
½ tsp. salt	2 Tbsp. each, butter and cooking oil
⅛ tsp. pepper	1 cup shredded cheddar cheese
½ cup chopped meat (jerky, dry salami, ham or cooked bacon)	

Beat eggs, sour cream, salt and pepper well or mix in a blender. Cook meat, onions and potatoes in butter and oil until onion is tender and potatoes lightly browned.

Pour egg mixture over all, lifting potatoes to let eggs run under. Cook slowly in a covered fry pan until eggs are set, 8 to 10 minutes. Sprinkle with cheese and serve.

MAKES 3 OR 4 SERVINGS.

WILD BLUEBERRY PANCAKES

1	cup all-purpose flour	1¼ tsp. baking powder	2	eggs	½	cup milk
1	Tbsp. sugar	½ tsp. baking soda	1	cup sour cream or half-and-half	¾ to 1 cup blueberries
		¼ tsp. salt			Vegetable oil

Combine flour, sugar, baking powder, baking soda and salt in a mixing bowl. Beat eggs, sour cream and milk together. Add to flour mixture, beating until smooth.

Heat griddle over medium heat. Lightly coat with oil. Pour a scant ½ cup batter onto griddle; spread batter to make 5 to 6-inch circles. Sprinkle a few blueberries over. When bubbles form and break on top and edges lose their wet and shiny look (about 1 minute), flip pancake. Cook second side until brown and baked through (about 1 minute). Continue until all batter is used. Serve pancakes with warm Blueberry Sauce.

MAKES 4 SERVINGS.

Blueberry Sauce: Purée ½ cup blueberries in a small food processor or blender with 2 Tbsp. fresh lemon juice. Combine puréed blueberries ½ cup sugar, ½ cup water and ½ cinnamon stick in medium saucepan. Bring to a full boil, reduce heat and simmer 5 to 8 minutes. Add 1 cup blueberries and simmer 2 to 3 minutes, adding more sugar if needed. Discard cinnamon stick. Keep warm, pour over pancakes.

Chicken Fried Steak

2½ to 3 lbs. round steak
1   5-ounce can evaporated milk
2   Tbsp. green Tabasco® sauce
½   tsp. salt
2   cups all-purpose
    flour, divided
2   tsp. paprika
¾   tsp. garlic powder
1   tsp. each, salt and
    cracked pepper
Vegetable oil

Trim steak and pound, if needed, to ½-inch thick; cut into 6 to 8 pieces.

Combine milk, Tabasco® sauce and salt in a bowl. Measure 1 cup of flour into a bowl. Combine remaining flour, paprika, garlic powder, salt and pepper in another bowl.

Dip steak into flour, into milk mixture, and then into seasoned flour. Set aside until all meat is coated.

Heat 1 or 2-inches of oil in a heavy fry pan. Fry meat until both sides are golden brown, about 2 minutes per side.

Drain on paper towels. Serve with cream gravy, mashed potatoes and biscuits.

MAKES 6 TO 8 SERVINGS.

Cream Gravy: *Pour off all but 6 Tbsp. of fat from fry pan; add 6 Tbsp. flour into pan (use any leftover seasoned flour) and blend well. Gradually stir in 2½ cups milk. Cook and stir over medium heat until thickened. Season with salt and pepper. Cover steaks with gravy when served.*

MAKES 2 CUPS.

Chili Parlors

SUNSET CHILI

4 lbs. ground lean beef or turkey
2 or 3 Tbsp. vegetable oil
2 28-ounce cans whole tomatoes in juice, cut up
2 15-ounce cans tomato sauce
2 cups light beer or water
$\frac{3}{4}$ cup Chili Seasoning Mix (see below)
2 28-ounce cans pinto beans, optional

In a large chili kettle, brown meat in oil, stirring occasionally. Add tomatoes, tomato sauce, beer and seasoning mix. Bring to a boil; cover and simmer for 45 minutes. Rinse beans; drain and add to chili mixture. Cover and simmer 15 to 20 minutes.
15 TO 20 SERVINGS

SEASONING MIX:

$\frac{1}{4}$ cup ground red chili pepper or cayenne
$\frac{1}{4}$ cup paprika
2 Tbsp. dried, minced onion
4 tsp. cumin seeds
2 tsp. dried oregano
2 tsp. salt
1 tsp. garlic powder
1 tsp. crushed dried red pepper

"NO-NAME CHILI"... it's noon on an August day in Arizonia in a bowl. To make 10-12 servings: 1/4 pound finely chopped suet, or 3 to 4 Tbsps. cooking oil; 6 lbs. lean beef, cut into 1/2" cubes; one cup chili powder; 2 Tbsps. ground cumin; 2 Tbsps. ground oregano; 1 Tbsp. salt; 1-2 Tbsps. cayenne pepper; 4 cloves garlic, minced; two qts. beef broth and/or water; 1/2 cup finely ground cornmeal; 1/2 cup cold water... If using suet, fry it in a large chili kettle until crisp. Add beef to hot fat, 1 lb. at a time, and cook- stirring often until browned. Remove and repeat with remaining beef; when everything's browned, return it all to the kettle; add seasonings and beef broth. Cover. Simmer 1 1/2 - 2 hours. Skim fat, if needed. Combine cornmeal with cold water and stir into chili. Simmer 30 min, stirring occasionally. Serve with plenty of ice cold refreshments.

SUNSET CAFE

A WARM WELCOME from ARIZONA

CYCLONE CHILI

2 lbs. beef chuck, cut into
  ½-inch cubes
2 to 4 Tbsp. olive oil
  4 to 6 fresh Jalapeño peppers
  1 medium onion,
    chopped
  2 cloves garlic, minced
  ½ sweet green pepper,
    chopped

8 or 10 tomatillos
1 8-ounce can tomato sauce
1½ cups beef broth
3 Tbsp. chopped fresh
  cilantro
1 Tbsp. paprika
2 tsp. crushed cumin seeds
½ to 1 tsp. salt
¼ tsp. cracked black pepper

Brown beef in hot oil in a large heavy kettle.

Dice Jalapeño peppers, discarding seeds and membrane. Add to beef with onion, garlic and green pepper.

Husk tomatillos, wash and chop. There should be about 1½ cups; add to beef mixture. Add tomato sauce, beef broth, cilantro, paprika, cumin seeds and seasonings; bring to a boil.

Reduce heat and simmer for about 2 hours, or until beef is very tender.

MAKES 4 OR 5 SERVINGS.

Tornado Chili: *Use Habañero chili peppers instead of Jalapeños. Jalapeño Cornbread; see recipe on page 23.*

CHILI PIT CHILI

4 slices smoked bacon
2 lbs. lean pork, cut into cubes
1½ cups chopped onion
2 large cloves garlic, minced
1 Tbsp. chili powder
1 tsp. dried oregano
¼ tsp. ground cumin
1 quart chicken broth
2 14½-ounce cans hominy, drained
6 Ancho chilies
2 10-ounce cans corn kernels, drained

In a large kettle, over medium heat, fry bacon until crisp; remove bacon. Pour off all but 2 or 3 Tbsp. bacon fat; add pork. Cook and stir until brown. Add onion and garlic; cook and stir until onion is tender. Crumble bacon and add with chili powder, oregano, cumin, chicken broth and drained hominy; bring to a boil. Wash dried ancho chili pods, remove stems and seeds; cut up with kitchen shears and add to pork mixture. Simmer 2 or 3 hours until flavors blend and mellow, adding chicken broth or water if needed. Add corn and heat. Pass flour tortillas.

MAKES 8 TO 10 SERVINGS.

Texas Postcard Chili

About a lb. of lean ground beef;
½ lb fresh hot sausage (more if you like); 1 chopped onion; 1 cut-up green pepper; couple big spoons chili powder; small spoonfuls of salt, oregano, ground cumin; BIG pinch garlic powder; one qt. tomato juice; two handfuls elbow macaroni.

Brown beef & sausage in a big frypan; add onion, green pepper, stir until done. Add seasonings & about 3 cups of the tomato juice. Cover, simmer. Boil macaroni for 5 min., pour off water & add to frypan. Let it all cook another 10-15 min., might need to add more tomato juice or water, if any gets dry. Then serve it up and stand back — this is GOOD! Feeds 8

Recipes To Go.

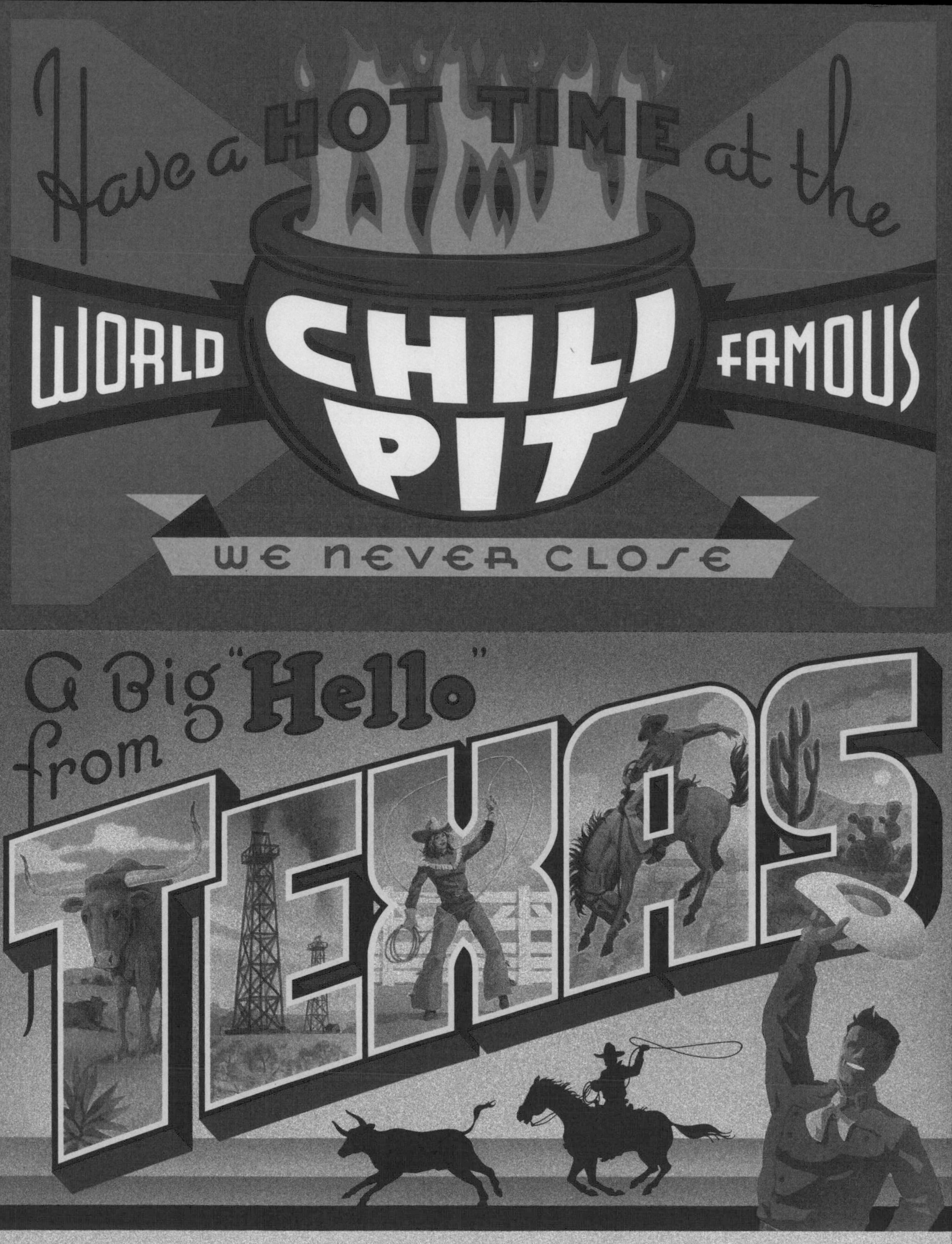

Name your **HEAT**

JALAPEÑO: where the fun begins!

PABLANO: BITES BACK

HABANERO: Teaches your tastebuds a lesson!!

VEGETARIAN CHILI

1 large onion, chopped
3 cloves garlic, minced
3 to 4 Tbsp. olive oil
1 cup chopped zucchini
1 cup chopped celery
1 cup chopped carrots
½ lb. mushrooms, chopped
½ cup chopped green pepper
2 16-ounce cans whole tomatoes, chopped
1 6-ounce can tomato paste
2 tsp. chili powder
1 tsp. salt
½ tsp. dried oregano
½ tsp. cumin seeds
2 16-ounce cans pinto beans

Cook onion and garlic in olive oil until tender; add chopped fresh vegetables; cook and stir for about 5 minutes. Add tomatoes and seasonings. Bring to a boil; cover and simmer 10 minutes until vegetables are tender but crisp.

Add beans and heat to boiling; simmer 5 minutes.

MAKES 6 TO 8 SERVINGS.

COWPOKE CHILI

2 lbs. dry pinto or red beans
Water
½ lb. smoked slab bacon
1 large onion, sliced
4 cloves garlic, sliced
2 Tbsp. chili powder

1 14½-ounce can whole tomatoes
12 Serrano chili peppers, seeded and finely chopped
1 tsp. coriander seeds, crushed
2 tsp. salt

Wash beans; put into a large pot or chili kettle. Pour over cold water to cover beans. Let stand overnight. Pour off the water and return beans to kettle.

Cut rind off bacon; add rind to beans. Chop bacon; set aside. Add onion, garlic and chili powder to beans; pour in 2 quarts water and bring to a boil. Cover and simmer beans for an hour or two, adding water if needed. Remove and discard bacon rind.

Fry chopped bacon, pouring off the fat. Add tomatoes, peppers and coriander to bacon; simmer about 10 minutes; add to the beans with salt. Simmer uncovered, for about 1 hour or until beans are tender.

For a thicker chili, mix about ¼ cup cornmeal with ½ cup cold water; add during the last half hour.

MAKES 15 TO 20 SERVINGS.

NUT AND SEED BREADSTICKS

1½ packages active dry yeast
2 cups lukewarm water
1 Tbsp. sugar
1½ tsp. salt
6 to 7 cups all-purpose flour

1 egg white
1 tsp. water
Coarse salt, sesame or poppy
seeds, ground nuts, grated
Parmesan cheese, etc.

Soften yeast in warm water; add sugar and salt; let stand until it is bubbly. Beat in flour, 1 cup at a time, until a smooth soft dough is formed. Turn out onto a floured surface; cover and let rest 5 minutes.

Knead, adding more flour as needed, until dough is smooth and elastic, about 10 minutes. Put dough into a large buttered bowl; turning it to butter top. Cover and let rise in a warm place until doubled, about 1½ to 2 hours. Turn out and punch down; knead lightly. Cover and let rest 5 minutes.

Cut dough into 3 parts. Roll each part into a rectangle, 15 x 9-inches, and cut into fifteen 9 x 1-inch strips. Roll strips between hands into thin pencils. Lay on greased baking sheets or breadstick pans.

With a fork, beat together egg white and 1 tsp. water. Brush over dough strips. Sprinkle with salt, seeds or selected topping. Repeat with remaining dough.

Place breadsticks in a cold oven. Put a pan of boiling water on rack under breadsticks. Turn on the oven to 400° and bake 12 to 15 minutes.

MAKES 45 BREADSTICKS.

JALAPEÑO CORNBREAD

1½ cups yellow cornmeal
1½ Tbsp. sugar
1½ tsp. salt
1½ cups milk
1 Tbsp. baking powder
1½ tsp. baking soda

2 eggs, slightly beaten
⅓ to ½ cup finely chopped
Jalapeño peppers
½ cup shredded Monterey
Jack or cheddar cheese
¼ cup chopped onion

Combine cornmeal, sugar and salt in a mixing bowl. Scald milk, pour over cornmeal; cool to lukewarm. Add remaining ingredients and mix well.

Pour into a well-greased 9-inch square or round baking pan. Bake in a 425° oven for 40 to 45 minutes.

MAKES 9 TO 12 SERVINGS.

CHILI SEASONING MIX

¼ cup ground red chili pepper
or cayenne
¼ cup paprika
2 Tbsp. dried minced onion
4 tsp. cumin seeds
2 tsp. dried oregano
2 tsp. salt
1 tsp. garlic powder
1 tsp. crushed dried red pepper

Combine all ingredients.
MAKES ¾ CUP.

Add 3 Tbsp. to each pound
of meat when making chili.
Replace commercial chili powder
in favorite recipes. Use to season
meat for tacos or taco salad. Add
to ground beef for grilled burgers
or a meat loaf.

1. Dried red pepper 2. Ancho & Guajillo
3. Paprika 4. Cayenne 5. Crushed
dried red pepper 6. Dried oregano
7. Finger peppers 8. Habañero
9. Crushed dried red pepper 10. The Mix

Pool Halls

TEXAS BEEF ON TEXAS TOAST

1	red or green sweet pepper	1	small clove garlic, pressed
1	ripe tomato		
2	Tbsp. olive oil		Dash cayenne
1	tsp. Dijon-style mustard	8	thick slices of High Country Loaf (see page 85)
1	Tbsp. chopped parsley, optional		
3 to 4	Tbsp. soft butter or margarine	1 to 1¼	lbs. sliced cooked roast beef or sandwich steaks

Chop or slice pepper into big pieces. Slice tomato.
Quickly cook pepper and tomato slices in olive oil; stir in mustard and parsley.
Combine butter, garlic and cayenne; spread on bread. Grill or broil buttered bread.
Put sliced roast beef on top of grilled bread; spoon pepper mixture over meat. Top with second slice of toast. If using sandwich steaks, grill or sauté in butter before making sandwich.
MAKES 4 SERVINGS.

PIZZA CALIFORNIA STYLE

1½ cups whole wheat flour
½ to 1 tsp. salt
1½ tsp. active dry yeast
½ cup lukewarm water
1 Tbsp. olive oil
12 medium-small plum tomatoes, oven roasted (see page 124)
1 cup chopped onion
3 Tbsp. chopped fresh basil
1 medium zucchini, thinly sliced lengthwise
2 cups shredded cheese (mozzarella, Monterey Jack, colby, etc.)

Combine flour and salt in a food processor or mixing bowl. Soften yeast in lukewarm water; let stand until bubbly.

Turn on the food processor and pour in softened yeast and olive oil. Process until a ball forms. If mixing by hand, stir yeast and oil into flour; turn onto a lightly floured surface and knead until smooth, 5 to 8 minutes.

Brush dough ball with oil; cover tightly or place in a plastic bag, leaving space for dough to rise. Refrigerate for several hours or overnight.

Remove dough from refrigerator. Let stand at room temperature 5 to 10 minutes.

Pour oil and juice from the tomatoes into a fry pan; add onion and cook until tender; adding more oil if needed. Stir in chopped basil and cool.

Flatten dough and roll into a 12 or 14-inch round. Place on a large, greased baking sheet; turn up the edges slightly.

Spread cooked onion mixture over dough; top with sliced zucchini and roasted tomatoes, cut side up.

Place on lowest rack in a 450° oven; bake for 20 minutes. Remove from oven and sprinkle with cheese. Return to oven and bake for 5 minutes more.

MAKES 6 TO 8 SERVINGS.

RED HOT POKER POTATOES

4 medium baking potatoes
4 long, thin red or green chili peppers
Salt
Vegetable oil
Melted butter, optional
Cracked pepper

Scrub and dry potatoes. Using an apple corer, make a hole lengthwise through center of each potato. Sprinkle salt in the hole.

Wash and dry peppers, push one into each potato. Coat potato skins with oil.

Bake in a 350° oven for 1 to 1½ hours or until done.

To serve, break open potato and serve with melted butter and cracked pepper.

MAKES 4 SERVINGS.

CHOPPED STEAK SPECIAL

1½ lbs. ground sirloin
3 Tbsp. grated or minced onion
1 Tbsp. minced chili pepper
1 tsp. salt

1 tsp. spicy steak or Worcestershire sauce
¼ tsp. green or red Tabasco® sauce

Combine all ingredients until well mixed. Shape into four fat oval patties. Pan broil in a heavy skillet; broil 3 to 5-inches from heat, or grill over medium coals. Cook 5 to 7 minutes per side or to desired doneness.

MAKES 4 STEAKS.

PINTO BEANS

1 lb. dried pinto beans
Water
2 cloves garlic, minced
2 onions finely chopped
⅓ cup finely chopped Jalapeño peppers, seeds removed

1 Tbsp. sugar
1 tsp. ground cumin
¼ tsp. black pepper
1 tsp. salt
¾ cup finely chopped smoked bacon or salt pork

Wash beans; put into a large bowl or cooking pot. Pour water over beans to cover; let stand overnight. Drain and discard water.

Put beans, garlic, onions, peppers, sugar, cumin and pepper into a large cooking pot. Pour 6 cups of water over mixture. Bring to a boil and simmer 45 minutes.

Add salt and bacon; continue to simmer until beans are tender, about 45 minutes.

MAKES 8 TO 10 SERVINGS.

GREEN CHILI CHEESE SQUARES

1 4-ounce can chopped green chilies
1 cup shredded Monterey Jack cheese

1 cup shredded sharp cheddar cheese
¼ cup minced onion
¼ cup crumbled potato chips

8 eggs, slightly beaten
½ cup milk
Dash cayenne
Chopped cilantro or parsley

Mix chilies, cheeses and onion; put in bottom of a well greased 8-inch square baking pan. Sprinkle crumbled potato chips over all. Combine eggs, milk and cayenne; pour over chips, chilies and cheese.
Bake in a 325° oven for 45 to 50 minutes or until set. Cool 5 minutes. Cut into shapes and serve with toothpicks. Sprinkle with chopped cilantro or parsley, if desired. Serve warm or at room temperature.
MAKES ABOUT 3 DOZEN APPETIZERS.

It's the

coffee that

wakes up

all the flavor

in this stew.

BLACK JAVA BEEF STEW

3	lbs. lean beef	¼	tsp. pepper
¼	cup vegetable oil	1¼	cup dry red wine
1	large onion, sliced	¾	cup strong black coffee
¼	cup all-purpose flour	3	cloves garlic, minced
1	tsp. salt	¾	tsp. dried thyme

In a heavy pan, brown meat; remove meat from pan. Cook onion in hot oil.

Combine flour, salt and pepper; toss with browned meat. Return to pan; cook and stir to brown flour.

Add wine, coffee, garlic and thyme. Cover and simmer for 2 hours. Lift out cooked meat and onions with a slotted spoon.

Boil sauce to thicken. Adjust seasonings. Return meat and onion; heat.

Serve with sautéed sliced mushrooms, if desired.

MAKES 6 TO 8 SERVINGS.

Watering Holes

TRAIL MIX

2 lbs. peanuts (dry roasted, etc.)
1 8½-ounce pkg. pretzel chips
1 7-ounce pkg. small twisted pretzels
1 5¾-ounce pkg. thin pretzel sticks
1 5.6-ounce pkg. corn nuts
1 cup vegetable oil
1 cup melted butter
2 Tbsp. chili powder
2 Tbsp. Worcestershire sauce
5 drops green Tabasco®
   sauce
1 Tbsp. garlic salt
1 Tbsp. seasoned salt
1 tsp. ground cumin

Mix nuts and pretzels
in a large roasting pan.
Mix oil and melted butter,
chili powder, Worcestershire,
Tabasco® sauce, garlic salt, seasoned salt
and cumin; pour over pretzels, mixing well.
Bake in a 250° oven for 2 hours,
stirring often.

MAKES 5½ QUARTS.

Note: For variety,
add chocolate covered raisins.

GUACAMOLE

1½ cups mashed ripe
    avocados
2 Tbsp. minced onion
1 Tbsp. lemon juice
1 to 2 Tbsp. finely chopped
    green chili pepper

¾ tsp. salt
½ tsp. Worcestershire sauce
4 drops Tabasco® sauce
1 clove garlic, minced
1 large ripe tomato, peeled,
    seeded and chopped

Combine avocado, onion, lemon juice, chili peppers, salt, Worcestershire, Tabasco® sauce and garlic. Cook tomato in a dry skillet until moisture is absorbed and tomato pieces turn light brown; cool before adding to avocado mixture.

MAKES
1¾ CUPS.

SOPAIPILLAS

4 cups all-purpose flour
1 Tbsp. baking powder
2 tsp. salt

¼ cup shortening
1⅓ cups milk or water
Vegetable oil

Mix flour, baking powder and salt in a mixing bowl. Cut in shortening; add milk and mix to make a soft dough. Knead until smooth, 5 minutes. Cover and let rest for 30 minutes.

Divide into 4 portions; keep covered except when rolling out. Roll each portion ⅛-inch thick; cut into nine 4x2-inch pieces. Cover while rolling and cutting remaining dough.

Heat 1-inch of oil in a heavy fry pan or deep fat fryer (375°). Fry 1 or 2 at a time, turning once, until brown and puffy, 4 to 5 minutes. Drain.

MAKES ABOUT 3 DOZEN.

Spicy Sopaipillas: Dust with chili powder. *Sweet Sopaipillas:* Dust with powdered sugar or break and fill with honey.

BEER BATTER FRIED ONION RINGS

1 cup all-purpose flour
1 tsp. salt
1 12-ounce can light beer
¼ to ½ tsp. red or green Tabasco® sauce
3 large Spanish onions
Flour
Vegetable oil

Combine flour, salt and beer; let stand until light and bubbly. Add Tabasco® sauce and let stand several hours or overnight.

Cut onions into ½-inch slices; separate into rings. Dip in flour, into beer batter and then in flour again.

Heat at least 1-inch oil in a large pot or deep fat fryer (375°). Fry battered onions, a few at a time, until golden brown, about 2 minutes, turning once.

MAKES 4 TO 6 SERVINGS.

Note: Mushrooms, peppers or other vegetables may be fried as directed.

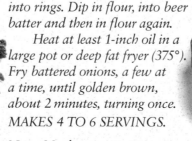

RED SALSA WITH BAKED CHIPS

2 to 4 Tbsp. finely chopped onion   3   large ripe tomatoes   1 to 2 Tbsp. lemon or lime juice
2   cloves garlic, minced   2 to 4 Serrano peppers, minced   Salt and pepper
                                                   2 to 4 Tbsp. minced cilantro

Put chopped onion and garlic into a strainer and pour 2 cups boiling water over them; drain thoroughly; discard water. Cool. Peel tomatoes, remove seeds, chop.

Combine tomatoes with onion, garlic, peppers, cilantro, lemon juice, salt and pepper; refrigerate to allow flavors to blend.

MAKES ABOUT 2 CUPS.

Serve with Baked Chips; see recipe on page 42.

Green Salsa

10 to 12 medium-large tomatillos
3 cloves garlic, chopped
½ tsp. salt
3 Tbsp. water
1 or 2 fresh or marinated
   Jalapeño chili peppers
⅓ to ½ cup minced cilantro
2 Tbsp. vegetable oil

Husk tomatillos, wash, remove stem end and chop, about 3 cups. Set 1 cup aside.

Combine 2 cups chopped tomatillos with garlic, salt and water in a saucepan; cook until soft, about 15 minutes.

Cool slightly.

Press through a food mill or purée in food processor or blender. Remove stems, seeds and membrane from fresh peppers, chop. Add pepper, cilantro and oil; stir or purée. Finely chop reserved tomatillos and add. If using food processor, add and chop quickly.

MAKES ABOUT 1½ CUPS.

BUFFALO BURGER BUNS

1	recipe Nut and Seed Breadsticks dough (see page 23)	1	egg white
		1	tsp. water
			Yellow cornmeal

After dough has risen and been punched down, shape into 6 or 8 large buns. Place on a baking sheet that has been greased and sprinkled with cornmeal. Let rest 5 minutes.

Lightly beat together the egg white and water; brush over buns. Sprinkle tops with cornmeal. With a sharp knife, slash tops, if desired.

Place in a cold oven. Put a pan of boiling water in rack under loaves. Turn oven temperature to 400°. Bake buns for 20 to 25 minutes or until done.

MAKES 6 TO 8 BUNS.

BUFFALO BURGERS

½	cup butter, softened	1	green onion, finely chopped
2	Tbsp. chopped cilantro	1	small hot red pepper, minced
	and/or parsley	2	lbs. lean ground bccf or buffalo

Combine butter, chopped cilantro, parsley, onion and red pepper. On waxed paper or plastic wrap, shape into a cylinder, 1-inch diameter and 8-inch round. Wrap and freeze.

Shape meat into 6 large balls. Cut six ¾-inch lengths of the frozen butter. Freeze remaining butter for another day.

Make a depression into the center of the meat; place a frozen butter patty into each meatball and seal inside the meat.

Shape into patties, about 1-inch thick, being careful not to expose the butter. Broil or grill, 4-inches from the heat. Cook 4 to 5 minutes on each side.

Serve on burger buns with Fried Peppers and Onions (see page 42).

MAKES 6 BURGERS.

Fajita Steak

2	skirt or flank steaks, about 1 lb. each	1	tsp. ground cumin	12	flour tortillas
2	cloves garlic	1	tsp. crumbled dry oregano	¾	to 1 cup sour cream
2	tsp. salt			¾	to 1 cup guacamole
½	tsp. black pepper	2	Tbsp. olive oil	1	recipe Red Salsa (see page 38)
		1	cup lime juice (6-8 limes)		

If using flank steak, score it before cutting into 5 or 6-inch lengths. Mash garlic and seasonings together; add olive oil. Rub on both sides of the steak.

Put a single layer of steak in a rectangular glass baking dish. Pour lime juice over all, lifting meat to make certain all meat is coated. Marinate for 30 minutes.

Grill over hot coals or broil, 3 inches from heat source, for 4 or 5 minutes on each side.

To serve, cut into thin strips. Roll up in flour tortillas; dress with sour cream, guacamole and salsa.

MAKES 6 SERVINGS.

Fried Peppers and Onions

1	sweet green pepper, sliced	1 to 2 Tbsp. vegetable oil	Salt and pepper
1	medium onion, sliced	1 to 2 Tbsp. beef broth or pan drippings	¼ tsp. fresh or
1	clove garlic, minced	1 Tbsp. red wine	⅛ tsp. dried thyme

Fry pepper, onion and garlic in oil until lightly browned. Add beef broth and red wine; simmer until onion is soft, about 3 minutes. Season with salt, pepper and thyme.

MAKES 4 SERVINGS.

Potato Skins

3	Idaho russet baking potatoes	Salt, pepper, paprika or cayenne
	Vegetable oil	2	Tbsp. grated Parmesan cheese
3 or 4 Tbsp. olive oil			
1 to 2 cloves garlic, minced	1 to 2 Tbsp. minced parsley

Wash and scrub potatoes; pat dry. Rub potato skins with oil.

Bake in a 425° oven for 1½ hours or until done. Remove potatoes from oven; cool.

Cut in half and carefully scoop out centers, leaving about ¼ to ½-inch layer of cooked potato. Cut each half potato skin into 3 lengthwise wedges. Place on baking sheet; brush insides of potatoes generously with olive oil. Sprinkle with garlic, seasonings, cheese and parsley.

Return to oven and bake for 20 to 25 minutes until crisp and lightly browned.

MAKES 18 PIECES.

Baked Chips

10 to 12 flour tortillas
Vegetable oil or spray pancoat
Seasoned salt, chili powder, etc.
Cinnamon sugar spiked with chili powder

Cut tortillas into 8 wedges.

Brush a shallow baking pan with oil or spray it with pancoat. Arrange tortillas in a single layer on pan. Brush them lightly with oil. Sprinkle with desired seasoning. Bake in a 325° oven until crisp and lightly browned.

MAKES 80 TO 96 CHIPS.

Hotels

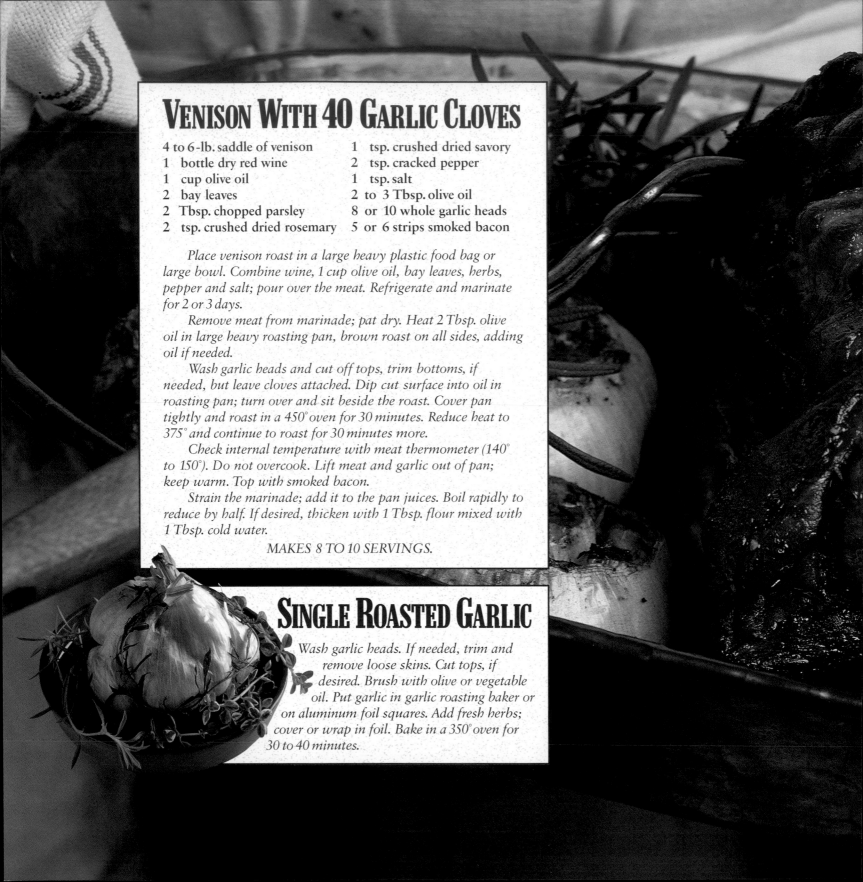

VENISON WITH 40 GARLIC CLOVES

4 to 6-lb. saddle of venison	1 tsp. crushed dried savory
1 bottle dry red wine	2 tsp. cracked pepper
1 cup olive oil	1 tsp. salt
2 bay leaves	2 to 3 Tbsp. olive oil
2 Tbsp. chopped parsley	8 or 10 whole garlic heads
2 tsp. crushed dried rosemary	5 or 6 strips smoked bacon

Place venison roast in a large heavy plastic food bag or large bowl. Combine wine, 1 cup olive oil, bay leaves, herbs, pepper and salt; pour over the meat. Refrigerate and marinate for 2 or 3 days.

Remove meat from marinade; pat dry. Heat 2 Tbsp. olive oil in large heavy roasting pan, brown roast on all sides, adding oil if needed.

Wash garlic heads and cut off tops, trim bottoms, if needed, but leave cloves attached. Dip cut surface into oil in roasting pan; turn over and sit beside the roast. Cover pan tightly and roast in a 450° oven for 30 minutes. Reduce heat to 375° and continue to roast for 30 minutes more.

Check internal temperature with meat thermometer (140° to 150°). Do not overcook. Lift meat and garlic out of pan; keep warm. Top with smoked bacon.

Strain the marinade; add it to the pan juices. Boil rapidly to reduce by half. If desired, thicken with 1 Tbsp. flour mixed with 1 Tbsp. cold water.

MAKES 8 TO 10 SERVINGS.

SINGLE ROASTED GARLIC

Wash garlic heads. If needed, trim and remove loose skins. Cut tops, if desired. Brush with olive or vegetable oil. Put garlic in garlic roasting baker or on aluminum foil squares. Add fresh herbs; cover or wrap in foil. Bake in a 350° oven for 30 to 40 minutes.

3 POTATOES IN A POT

2 large white potatoes	½ cup melted butter
2 medium sweet potatoes	3 Tbsp. grated
3 or 4 medium redskin potatoes	Parmesan cheese*
	Salt and pepper

Wash and pare white and sweet potatoes; wash redskin potatoes, do not pare. Cut all into thin slices. Keep potatoes in salted water as you work. There should be 2 cups of each potato.

Brush the bottom and sides of a 12x8-inch baking dish with melted butter; sprinkle with cheese. Drain and dry potatoes. Arrange 6 layers of potato slices in baking dish in this order: white; sweet; redskin. Brush each layer with melted butter and sprinkle with salt and pepper. End with redskin potatoes.

Cover baker tightly with aluminum foil. Bake in a 350° oven for 45 minutes. Carefully remove foil and continue baking for 30 minutes, until potatoes are brown and tender.

MAKES 6 TO 8 SERVINGS.

Additional cheese may be sprinkled between potato layers, if desired.

BOILED & BAKED NEW POTATOES

1½ lbs. redskin potatoes
¼ cup melted butter
Garlic salt
Cayenne
Dried thyme or rosemary
Black pepper
1 to 2 Tbsp. shredded Parmesan cheese

Wash potatoes. If small, leave whole; if large, cut into halves or quarters. Steam or boil until almost done, 10 to 20 minutes. Drain and cool slightly.

Roll potatoes in melted butter and arrange in a single layer in a shallow baking pan. Sprinkle with garlic salt, cayenne, thyme and pepper.

Bake in a 425° oven for 20 minutes, turning once or twice. Sprinkle with Parmesan cheese and bake until cheese browns, about 10 minutes.

MAKES 4 TO 6 SERVINGS.

For Asparagus with Brown Butter;
see recipe page 53.
For Stuffed Pork Chops;
see recipe page 52.

Split Pea Soup

1 lb. dried yellow or green peas
2 quarts water
1 small smoked ham hock
1 lb. fresh pork neck bones
1 onion stuck with 4 or 5 whole cloves
2 cloves garlic, minced
1 bay leaf
½ tsp. dried thyme or marjoram
1 cup chopped carrots
⅓ cup chopped celery
½ tsp. salt
¼ tsp. black pepper

Rinse the dried peas; drain. Put into a large soup pot, cover with water and bring to a boil; simmer 1 hour. If using yellow peas, remove shells that float to the top.

Put ham hock and fresh pork into a large cooking pot, cover with water; bring to a boil. Lift out meat and discard water. Add meat to peas with onion, garlic, bay leaf and thyme; bring to a boil and simmer for 1½ hours.

Remove the pork, onion and bay leaf; discard onion and bay leaf. Cut meat from bones; discard bones and skin. Chop meat and return to soup. Add chopped vegetables. Season with salt and pepper. Simmer until vegetables are tender, about 10 minutes. Add more water, if needed.

MAKES 6 TO 8 SERVINGS.

Mexican Tomato Soup

18 oven-roasted plum tomatoes (see page 124)
⅓ cup finely chopped onion
2 Tbsp. olive oil
1 tsp. chili powder
¼ tsp. ground cumin
¼ tsp. salt
1¼ cups chicken broth
½ cup sour cream
2 Tbsp. tequila, optional
Sour cream
Sliced avocado
Blue corn tortilla chips

Remove roasted tomatoes from baking dish; put into food processor or blender.

Pour oil and pan juices from tomatoes into a medium fry pan. Add onion, chili powder, cumin and salt; cook and stir over medium heat until onion is soft, about 4 minutes. Add a small amount of chicken broth, if necessary.

Add cooked onion to tomatoes in food processor or blender. Purée, this may need to be done in batches. Press through a sieve or food mill to remove seeds and skin, if desired. You should have about 2 to 3 cups of tomato purée.

Combine purée, chicken broth and ½ cup sour cream; beat or blend until well mixed. May be served hot or at room temperature.

Add tequila and top each serving with a dollop of sour cream and avocado. Serve with blue corn tortilla chips.

MAKES 6 SERVINGS.

GREEN SOUP

8 cups loosely packed
  torn spring greens
  (spinach, watercress, etc.)
1 large baking potato,
  pared and sliced

1 small onion, sliced
3 cups chicken broth
1½ cups plain yogurt
Chopped toasted pine
  nuts, optional

Wash and chop greens; put into a large soup kettle with potato, onion and broth. Bring to a boil and simmer 20 minutes. Cool slightly.

Purée in a food processor or blender in small batches. Add yogurt to the last batch before blending. When finished, mix it all together.

Serve hot or cold topped with pine nuts. Swirl more yogurt through the soup before serving, if desired.

MAKES 5 OR 6 SERVINGS.

BEEF BARLEY MUSHROOM SOUP

3 lbs. beef shanks,
  oxtails or short ribs
3 Tbsp. olive oil
3 or 4 beef bones
1 15-ounce can whole
  tomatoes, cut up
1½ tsp. salt
Water
1 package (1 to 2 oz.)
  dried mushrooms,
  (porcinis, cépes,
  shiitake, etc.)

½ cup barley
1 cup dry red wine
1 cup water
1 cup, each, sliced
  carrots and
  green beans
½ cup diced celery
¼ cup chopped onion
Chopped fresh dill,
  optional

Brown beef shanks in hot oil in a large Dutch oven: add bones if available. Add tomatoes and salt; pour enough water over beef to cover, 4 to 6 cups. Bring to a boil, cover and simmer for 2 hours. Remove meat and bones; set aside to cool.

Cool broth and remove fat. This may be done the day before finishing soup. While broth is cooling, remove meat from the bones, discard bones. Chop the meat into bite-size pieces and set aside.

Rinse mushrooms and drain. Put mushrooms and barley in a bowl; cover with 1 cup red wine and 1 cup water, let stand 30 minutes. Cut up mushrooms, discarding tough stems.

Put skimmed broth (there should be about 6 cups), chopped meat, barley, mushrooms and wine into Dutch oven. Bring to a boil, cover and simmer for 45 minutes. Add prepared vegetables and simmer 15 minutes more. Adjust seasoning. Add chopped dill before serving.

MAKES 8 TO 10 SERVINGS.

5 Rib Roast

4 or 5 rib standing beef roast
¾ cup chopped onion
2 cloves garlic, minced
2 large chili peppers, minced
⅓ cup chopped parsley
Salt and pepper
2 cups dry red wine or
  beef broth

Have butcher cut meat from rib bones and backbone, discard backbone. Trim excess fat from roast if needed. Turn ribs up, tie the roast on top of ribs, leaving a space between meat and bones. (A butcher can do this.)

Combine onion, garlic, peppers and parsley; fill the hollow between ribs and meat with chopped vegetables. Place roast, rib side down, in shallow roasting pan. Sprinkle with salt and pepper.

Roast meat in a 450° oven for 30 minutes. Reduce heat to 350° and roast 30 minutes more.

Remove from oven and cut strings that tie meat to ribs. Lift meat off ribs and return to pan. Push vegetables off bones into pan around the meat; bones may be removed at this time, if desired.

Roast 30 to 60 minutes more. Check internal temperature with meat thermometer for desired doneness. 130°(rare), 150°(medium), 160°(well–not recommended). Remove meat from pan and let rest while making sauce.

Remove bones from pan; skim or pour off excess fat. Add red wine or broth to drippings. Bring to a boil and cook rapidly until reduced by ⅓ to ½, strain; discard vegetables and reduce again if desired. Adjust seasonings. Serve au jus with sliced beef.

MAKES 6 TO 8 SERVINGS.

Stuffed Pork Chops

2 Tbsp. diced smoked bacon
½ cup finely chopped onion
½ cup finely chopped
  tart apple
2 cloves garlic, minced
4 cups chopped spinach,
  lightly packed
1 Tbsp. apple cider vinegar
1 Tbsp. sugar
¼ tsp. salt
4 thick pork chops
Salt and pepper
2 to 4 Tbsp. vegetable oil
Hot water

Cook bacon, onion, apple and garlic together until tender and lightly browned. Add spinach; cook and stir until wilted. Add vinegar, sugar and salt to taste; cover and simmer for 5 minutes. Set aside.

Cut a pocket into each chop and fill with spinach stuffing. Season with salt and pepper. Heat 2 Tbsp. oil in a large heavy skillet. Brown chops 5 to 7 minutes on each side, adding oil if needed. Pour off excess fat.

Chops may be baked in skillet if it is large enough. Otherwise, arrange chops in a 13x9-inch baking dish; pour ¼-inch hot water around chops. Bake in a 350° oven for 1 hour.

MAKES 4 SERVINGS.

Asparagus With Brown Butter

1½ to 2 lbs. asparagus or broccoli   2   Tbsp. lemon juice
4 to 6 Tbsp. butter or margarine   ½   tsp. salt
¼ cup slivered almonds   ⅛   tsp. pepper

Wash and trim vegetables. Cook in boiling salted water until done, 8 to 12 minutes. Drain and keep warm.

Melt butter in a small saucepan or fry pan over medium heat. Add almonds; cook and stir until butter and almonds are golden brown, 1 or 2 minutes. Add lemon juice, salt and pepper. Spoon over hot asparagus.

MAKES 6 TO 8 SERVINGS.

Butter Stewed Carrots

1   lb. carrots   ½   tsp. sugar
6   Tbsp. butter or   ¼   tsp. salt
    margarine   ¼   tsp. white pepper

Wash, scrape and shred carrots. There should be about 4 cups. Cook carrots with butter in a large fry pan over medium-low heat, stirring occasionally. When carrots are tender, sprinkle with sugar, salt and pepper, tossing to mix well. These may be cooked ahead of time, then reheated before serving.

MAKES 4 SERVINGS.

Sour Cream Pound Cake

3   cups all-purpose   1   cup butter or   6   eggs
    flour   margarine, softened 1   cup sour cream
¼   tsp. baking soda   2½ cups sugar   2   tsp. vanilla

Sift together flour and baking soda twice to lighten flour. Set aside. Beat together butter and sugar; add eggs, one at a time, beating after each addition.

Add flour, alternately with sour cream, mixing well after each addition; end with flour. Stir in vanilla.

Grease two 9-inch loaf pans; line with parchment baking paper. Divide batter between pans.

Bake in a 350° oven for 1 hour 20 minutes or until done. Cool 15 minutes before turning out.

MAKES 12 TO 14 SERVINGS PER CAKE.

Lemon Pound Cake: Add 1 Tbsp. lemon juice and 1 tsp. grated lemon peel to the batter. Combine 1 cup sifted confectioners' sugar, 1 Tbsp. lemon juice and 1 Tbsp. whiskey, stirring until smooth. Spoon over warm baked cakes.

Bread Pudding

1   1-lb. loaf of raisin or cinnamon bread   1   cup sugar
4 to 6 Tbsp. soft butter or margarine   1½ tsp. vanilla
½   cup chopped pecans or walnuts   ¼   tsp. salt
4   eggs, beaten   3   cups milk, scalded

Spread sliced bread lightly with butter; stack 3 or 4 slices and cut into cubes or triangles. Put into a buttered 2½ or 3-quart baker; sprinkle with chopped nuts.

Beat together eggs, sugar, vanilla and salt until well mixed. Beat in hot milk; pour over bread, making certain all bread is coated with milk mixture.

Let stand at least 30 minutes until bread absorbs liquid. Bake in a 350° oven for 45 to 50 minutes or until set.

Cool slightly before serving. Spoon over Very Cool Whiskey Sauce, if desired.

MAKES 8 TO 10 SERVINGS.

Very Cool Whiskey Sauce: Stir together ½ pint softened vanilla ice cream and 1 Tbsp. whiskey. Add ½ cup whipped cream to softened ice cream.

MAKES ABOUT 1½ CUPS.

BERRIES'N BISCUITS SHORTCAKE

½ cup strawberry or red pepper jelly
¼ cup orange juice
2 pints strawberries
3 cups all-purpose flour
5 Tbsp. sugar
2 Tbsp. baking powder
¾ tsp. salt
¾ tsp. cream of tartar
1½ tsp. grated orange peel
¾ cup butter
1 cup milk
Melted butter
1 tsp. sugar
⅛ tsp. ground cardamom
1 Tbsp. finely chopped pecans

Combine jelly and orange juice; heat until jelly melts. Cool.

Wash berries and slice. Pour jelly mixture over sliced berries and refrigerate.

Mix together flour, 5 Tbsp. sugar, baking powder, salt, cream of tartar and orange peel in a mixing bowl; cut in butter until crumbly. Add milk and mix to make a soft dough. Turn out onto a buttered baking sheet and shape into an 8 or 9-inch round; pat top to smooth. Brush top with melted butter and sprinkle with a mixture of sugar, cardamom and pecans.

Bake in a 400° oven for 20 to 25 minutes or until lightly browned. Cool to room temperature.

To serve: Split shortcake and spoon berries over bottom half. Replace top and ladle over remaining berries. Serve with whipped cream.

MAKES 8 SERVINGS.

Bread Pudding;
see recipe on page 53.

Pound Cake;
see recipe on page 53.

CUSTARD PIE

Pastry for 1 pie shell   2½ cups milk,
  (see page 145)   scalded
½ cup sugar   1   cup flaked coconut
1   tsp. all-purpose flour   ¾   cup fresh fruit
¼   tsp. salt   (berries, pitted
4   eggs, slightly beaten   cherries, thinly
1   tsp. vanilla   sliced plums, etc.)

Roll pastry to fit a 10-inch pie plate. Shape and crimp edge to form a standing collar; refrigerate.

Mix sugar, flour and salt together in a bowl; stir in eggs and vanilla. Gradually add hot milk, beating to mix well; stir in coconut. Remove pie shell from refrigerator; sprinkle prepared fruit in bottom. Pour custard over fruit. Bake in a 400° oven for 35 to 40 minutes. Chill before cutting.

MAKES 6 TO 8 SERVINGS.

RANCH

Ranch Houses

Chicken Pot Pie

1½ cups sliced fresh mushrooms
1 cup red and/or green pepper strips
⅓ cup butter
½ cup all-purpose flour
½ tsp. salt
¼ tsp. each, pepper and paprika
3 cups chicken broth
½ cup milk or half-and-half
3 cups chopped cooked chicken
1 Tbsp. lemon juice
1 recipe Sage Biscuits (see below)

In a 10-inch oven-going fry pan, cook mushrooms and peppers in 1 Tbsp. butter until tender. Remove vegetables from pan.

Melt remaining butter in fry pan; stir in flour and seasonings. Add chicken broth and milk; cook and stir until mixture boils and thickens. Stir in chicken, vegetables and lemon juice. Keep hot in fry pan or 2½-quart casserole.

Prepare biscuits as directed in recipe; place wedges on top of hot chicken mixture. Bake in a 350° oven for 35 to 45 minutes or until biscuits are done.

MAKES 6 SERVINGS.

Sage Biscuits:

2 cups all-purpose flour
4 tsp. baking powder
1 tsp. salt
1 tsp. rubbed dried sage
½ tsp. cumin seed
6 Tbsp. shortening
¾ cup milk
2 tsp. light corn syrup
1 tsp. water

Combine flour, baking powder, salt, sage and cumin in mixing bowl. Cut in shortening until crumbly. Add milk and mix to moisten flour.

Shape into a ball; turn out onto a lightly floured surface. Roll or pat into an 8-inch circle. Cut into 6 wedges. Use as directed above.

May be cut with floured 2½-inch round cutter. Brush tops with mixture of syrup and water; place on an ungreased baking sheet.

Bake in a 450° oven for 12 minutes or until brown.

MAKES ABOUT 1 DOZEN.

VEGETABLE STEW

3	Tbsp. butter or margarine	1	tsp. fresh thyme leaves
2	large ripe tomatoes, peeled and chopped	½	tsp. chopped fresh rosemary
1	Tbsp. sugar	5	medium red potatoes
½	tsp. salt		
⅛ to ½	tsp. cayenne	2	cups sugar snap peas
½	cup heavy cream	4	large leaves red or green chard or 10 ounces fresh spinach
1	Tbsp. fresh lemon juice		
1	Tbsp. chopped fresh parsley		
1½	tsp. each, chopped fresh summer savory, basil and marjoram	2	cups small carrots or 1-inch slices
		2	cups chicken broth

Melt butter in a medium fry pan; add tomatoes; sprinkle over sugar, salt and cayenne. Cook over medium heat until mixture thickens. Cool.

Put through a food mill or purée. Beat in cream, lemon juice and herbs. Set aside.

Pare potatoes; cut into chunks. Trim peas. Wash chard and cut into ½-inch slices.

Heat broth in a large saucepan; add potatoes and carrots. Place peas on top. Bring to a boil, cover and cook slowly until done, 12 to 15 minutes. Lift out vegetables with slotted spoon; set aside. Add chard to hot broth; cover and cook 5 minutes, stir once. Remove chard. Combine drained vegetables and tomato mixture. Heat and serve.

MAKES 6 TO 8 SERVINGS.

BEEF AND BEER STEW

⅓ cup finely chopped
  salt pork or bacon
2½ to 3 lbs. beef stew meat
3 large onions, sliced
3 Tbsp. paprika

1 Tbsp. salt
1 tsp. ground nutmeg
1 tsp. dried marjoram
2 12-ounce cans beer
1 cup water

1 6-ounce can tomato paste
1 Tbsp. Worcestershire sauce
4 large potatoes, cubed
6 carrots or parsnips,
  thickly sliced

Cook salt pork in a large stewpot until rendered. Add meat; cook and stir over medium-high heat until lightly browned. Remove meat. Reduce heat to medium; add onions and cook until tender. Return meat to pot and add seasonings, beer, water, tomato paste and Worcestershire; stir to mix. Cover and simmer until beef is tender, about 1½ hours.

Add prepared vegetables; cover and simmer until vegetables are cooked, about 45 minutes.

MAKES 8 TO 10 SERVINGS.

HEADQUARTERS CHILI PIE

2 lbs. ground lean beef or turkey meat	1 10-ounce can diced tomatoes with chilies
1 large onion, thinly sliced	2 Tbsp. chili powder
2 cloves garlic, minced	¼ tsp. red pepper flakes
2 Tbsp. vegetable oil	1 tsp. crushed cumin seeds
2 14½-ounce cans whole tomatoes, cut up	1 cup beer
	1 15-ounce can pinto beans

In a large chili pot, lightly brown meat, onion and garlic in hot oil, stirring as needed. Add canned tomatoes, seasonings and beer. Bring to a boil; cover and simmer 45 minutes. Rinse and drain beans; add to beef mixture; simmer 20 minutes.

Spoon chili into a 3-quart casserole or a 13x9-inch baker. Heat in a 375° oven for 15 minutes.

Cornmeal Crust:

⅔ cup yellow cornmeal	2 eggs
1 cup all-purpose flour	3 Tbsp. melted butter or margarine
2 tsp. sugar	
1 tsp. baking powder	½ cup shredded colby or Monterey Jack cheese
¼ tsp. salt	
⅔ cup milk	

Combine cornmeal, flour, sugar, baking powder and salt in a mixing bowl. Beat milk and eggs together. Add to cornmeal with melted butter and cheese. Stir until well mixed.

Remove chili from oven and spoon cornmeal mixture evenly over the top. Return to oven and bake 30 to 35 minutes or until cornbread is browned.

MAKES 6 TO 8 SERVINGS.

Note: Use any chili recipe in place of Headquarters Chili.

Ranch House Tortilla Bake

1 cup chopped onion
4 Tbsp. butter or margarine
6 Tbsp. all-purpose flour
½ cup milk
⅓ cup sour cream or half-and-half
¾ cup Green Salsa (see page 39)

Salt and pepper
3 cups cubed cooked chicken
12 corn tortillas
1½ to 2 cups shredded CoJack cheese
¼ cup chopped cilantro or parsley

Cook onion in butter until soft; stir in flour. Add milk and sour cream, cooking and stirring until thickened; stir in salsa. Season to taste; stir in cubed chicken.

Line a buttered 12x8-inch baker with 6 tortillas; spoon in chicken mixture. Top with remaining tortillas; sprinkle over cheese.

Bake in a 375° oven for 30 to 45 minutes or until cheese melts and chicken filling is hot. Sprinkle with cilantro before serving.

MAKES 6 SERVINGS.

Spiced Peaches

2 16-ounce or one 29-ounce can cling peach halves
½ cup white or brown sugar
½ cup cider vinegar

6 whole cloves
3 whole allspice
1 2½-inch cinnamon stick

Drain peaches; reserving juice for another use. Combine sugar, vinegar and spices. Bring to a boil and simmer 5 minutes. Add peaches and simmer 5 minutes more.

Remove from heat and allow peaches to cool in liquid. Serve warm or cold as a meat accompaniment or salad.

MAKES 7 TO 8 SERVINGS.

Grilled Pepper Steak

1½ to 2 lbs. skirt steak
½ cup red wine vinegar
½ cup white grape or apple juice
¼ cup finely chopped onion
1 clove garlic, minced
2 Tbsp. rubbed dried sage
1 Tbsp. freshly ground black pepper

1 Tbsp. each, ground coriander and dry mustard
1 tsp. salt
1 cup olive oil
12 small-medium bulb onions and/or peppers
6 long metal or wooden skewers

Trim steak if needed; put into a glass or enamel bowl. Combine remaining ingredients, except whole onions and peppers; pour over steak, turning to coat with marinade. Cover and marinate at least 1 hour.

Remove steak from marinade, cut into 6 portions. Soak wooden skewers in water before using. Thread meat onto long skewers, weaving meat around onions and peppers as you proceed.

Cook over hot coals or broil, 3 to 4 inches from heat, 12 to 15 minutes, turning to cook all sides. Brush meat with marinade as it cooks.

MAKES 6 SERVINGS.

ROASTED CHICKEN

1	roasting chicken, 4 to 5½ lbs.		Salt and pepper
½	cup butter or margarine		2 or 3 green onions
2	cloves garlic, minced		2 or 3 sprigs celery leaves
½	cup minced green onion		Melted butter
1	cup seasoned dry	1	tsp. Margarita salt
	bread crumbs	2	Tbsp. tequila

Wash chicken, dry and set aside. Cook liver in 2 Tbsp. butter; mash with fork and cool. Cream remaining butter; add garlic, minced onion, bread crumbs and cooked liver; season to taste.

Sit chicken on its back; loosen skin from breast, thigh and leg using fingers. Carefully fill area with butter mixture, patting skin down to spread butter evenly. Fill chicken cavity with green onion and celery leaves. Using kitchen string, tie legs and wings close to the chicken body to keep from overcooking. Cavity may be closed using poultry lacing pins.

Baste with melted butter. Bake in 375° oven for 2 to 2½ hours or until done. Combine salt and tequila; baste bird every 5 minutes during last 20 minutes cooking time. Tent with aluminum foil if bird browns too rapidly. Cook giblets to make broth for gravy, if desired.

MAKES 4 TO 6 SERVINGS.

Apple Pecan Dumplings

Pastry for 3 pie shells (see page 145)
2 oranges
½ cup light brown sugar, packed
¾ cup sugar, divided
1 Tbsp. all-purpose flour
4 medium cooking apples
½ tsp. cinnamon
2 to 3 Tbsp. cold butter or margarine
2 Tbsp. broken pecans

Wrapping stacked apple slices in pastry squares.

Grate 2 Tbsp. orange peel; squeeze orange juice, measure and add water to make 1 cup.

In a saucepan, mix ½ cup of each sugar with flour; add grated orange peel and juice. Cook and stir until mixture thickens and clears, about 3 minutes.

Pare, core and cut apples into 3 horizontal slices. Mix ¼ cup sugar and cinnamon; cut cold butter into 6 pieces.

Roll pastry ⅛-inch thick; cut into six 7-inch squares. Place 1 apple slice on each; sprinkle 1 tsp. cinnamon sugar. Top with second apple slice; press 1 piece butter into center of apples; sprinkle with cinnamon sugar.

Brush pastry edges with water; wrap around apples; pinch to seal. Place dumplings in 13x9-inch baking dish. Bake in a 400° oven for 10 minutes. Reduce oven temperature to 325°.

Spoon some orange sauce over dumplings; bake 10 minutes. Spoon over more sauce; bake 10 minutes. Repeat, sprinkling with pecans; bake 15 minutes.

MAKES 6 SERVINGS.

Double Apple Cake

2 cups all-purpose flour
1 tsp. baking soda
1 tsp. baking powder
1 tsp. ground cardamom
½ tsp. ground nutmeg
¼ tsp. ground cloves
¼ tsp. salt
3 eggs
¾ cup brown sugar, packed
¾ cup sugar
1 cup vegetable oil
2 cups shredded cooking apples
½ to 1 cup chopped walnuts
4 cups thinly sliced cooking apples

Combine flour, baking soda, baking powder, spices and salt. Beat eggs and sugars together, until well mixed.

Continue beating as you slowly pour in the oil. Add dry ingredients, beating to mix thoroughly. Stir in shredded apples and nuts.

Arrange sliced apples in bottom of a buttered 13x9-inch baking pan. Pour apple cake batter over sliced apples. A few apple slices may be sprinkled over top of batter, if desired.

Bake in a 350° oven for 1 hour. Serve with whipped cream if desired.

MAKES 12 SERVINGS.

Note: Winter pears may be used instead of apples.

Cookhouses

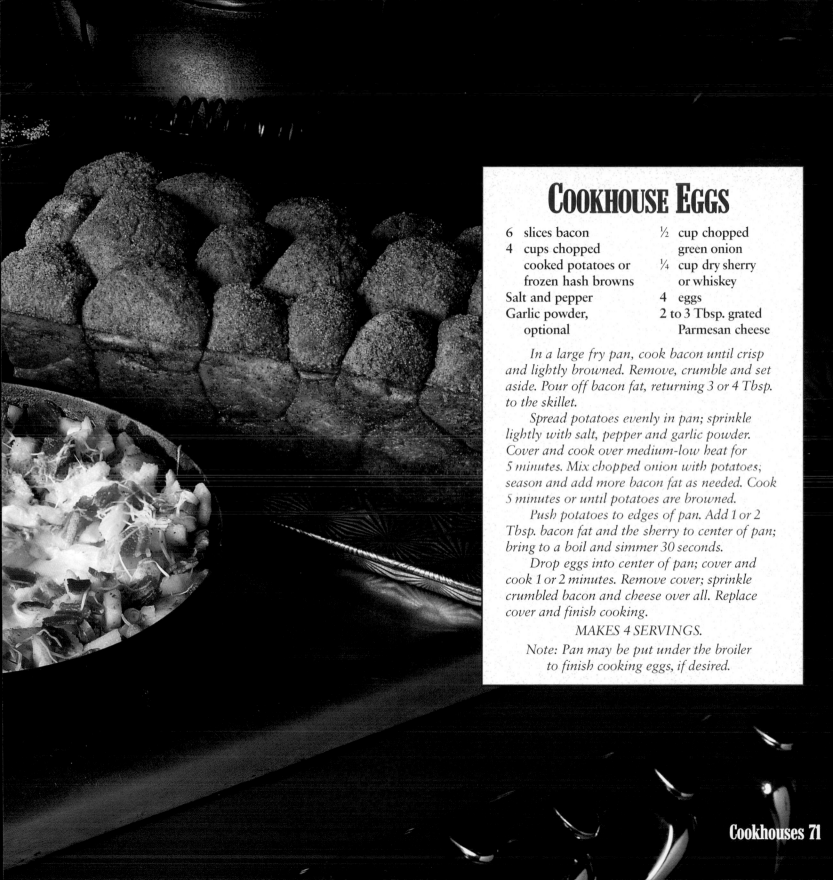

Cookhouse Eggs

6 slices bacon	½ cup chopped
4 cups chopped	green onion
cooked potatoes or	¼ cup dry sherry
frozen hash browns	or whiskey
Salt and pepper	4 eggs
Garlic powder,	2 to 3 Tbsp. grated
optional	Parmesan cheese

In a large fry pan, cook bacon until crisp and lightly browned. Remove, crumble and set aside. Pour off bacon fat, returning 3 or 4 Tbsp. to the skillet.

Spread potatoes evenly in pan; sprinkle lightly with salt, pepper and garlic powder. Cover and cook over medium-low heat for 5 minutes. Mix chopped onion with potatoes; season and add more bacon fat as needed. Cook 5 minutes or until potatoes are browned.

Push potatoes to edges of pan. Add 1 or 2 Tbsp. bacon fat and the sherry to center of pan; bring to a boil and simmer 30 seconds.

Drop eggs into center of pan; cover and cook 1 or 2 minutes. Remove cover; sprinkle crumbled bacon and cheese over all. Replace cover and finish cooking.

MAKES 4 SERVINGS.

Note: Pan may be put under the broiler to finish cooking eggs, if desired.

BEEF LOAF

1½ cups finely crushed corn chips
1   cup milk
1½ lbs. lean ground beef
2   cups Red Salsa, divided
    (see page 38)
2   eggs, beaten
2   Tbsp. chopped cilantro
    or parsley

Soak the corn chips in milk until soft; combine with beef, 1 cup salsa and eggs. Pack into a loaf pan or shape into a loaf in a shallow baking dish.

Combine remaining salsa and cilantro and spoon over the meat loaf. Bake in a 350° oven for 1 hour. Serve with additional salsa, if desired.

MAKES 6 TO 8 SERVINGS.

CHOPPED SALAD

1   cup each, chopped onion,
    tomato, cucumber, red and/or
    green sweet pepper
1   cup chopped tart apple
3 to 4 Tbsp. lemon juice
⅓ cup olive oil
Salt or seasoning salt
Pepper

Mix chopped vegetables and apple together in a mixing bowl. Combine remaining ingredients; pour over vegetables and apple. Toss. Refrigerate to allow flavors to blend.
MAKES 6 TO 8 SERVINGS.

BEEF STEAK TOMATOES WITH GARDEN HERBS

4   green onions, finely chopped
1   clove garlic, minced or crushed
1   tsp. minced hot chili pepper
    (Serrano, Jalapeño, etc.)
2 to 3 Tbsp. fresh lemon juice
3   Tbsp. olive oil
½ cup plain yogurt
Salt and pepper
1   cup lightly packed mixed
    garden herbs (parsley, chives,
    basil, marjoram, etc.)
4   beef steak tomatoes
1   sweet onion, sliced

Combine green onion, garlic, chilies and lemon juice. Beat in olive oil and yogurt gradually. Add salt and pepper. Finely chop herbs and add. This may be done in a food processor or blender. Refrigerate.

Serve over sliced tomatoes and onions.
MAKES 8 SERVINGS.

ORIGINAL SAN ANTONE CHILI

¼ lb. suet or pork fat
2 lbs. lean beef shoulder
1 lb. lean pork shoulder
¾ cup all-purpose flour
1 tsp. salt
½ tsp. cracked pepper
4 cups chopped onion
6 cloves garlic, minced

1½ quarts beef broth and water
4 Chili Ancho (dried Pablano)
1 Chili Pasilla (dried Chilaca)
1 Chili Cascabel, Catarina or
   Guajillo pepper
1½ cups water
1 Tbsp. crushed
   cumin seeds

Fry suet or fat in a 6 or 8-quart kettle until rendered; remove suet and discard. Cut meat into cubes.

Combine flour, salt and pepper in a brown paper bag. Add meat and shake to coat. Save remaining flour mixture.

Brown meat in hot fat, stirring to prevent sticking. Add onion and garlic; cook and stir until vegetables are tender.

Add beef broth and water; bring to a boil; cover and simmer slowly while preparing peppers.

Wash peppers under cold running water and dry. Remove stems and seeds; discard. Put peppers into a medium saucepan; add 1½ cups water and boil for 5 minutes. Remove from heat and let stand for 10 minutes.

Lift out peppers, reserving cooking water. Purée peppers in food processor or blender, adding pepper water as needed. Cumin seeds may be added to peppers for further grinding.

Add puréed peppers and cooking water to the meat; cover and simmer 1½ to 2 hours, until meat is very tender. Adjust seasonings, adding salt if needed.

If desired, thicken chili with a mixture of 2 to 4 Tbsp. reserved flour mixed with ¼ cup cold water; stir into meat mixture and simmer until thickened.

MAKES 10 TO 12 SERVINGS.

CHILI PASILLA
Slender and almost black, this dried chili is hot and strong. If unavailable, use 2 to 3 Tbsp. dark chili powder.

CHILI GUAJILLO
Smooth and shiny, this dried chili has a vicious bite. Can substitute ¼ to ½ tsp. cayenne to add the heat, if not the same taste.

Big Spread Bread

1   16-ounce package hot roll mix
1 to 1½ tsp. cracked black pepper
1 to 2 Tbsp. olive oil
2   cups shredded cheese (CoJack, Monterey Jack, colby, pepper cheese, etc.)
1   cup chopped meat (salami, ham, jerky, etc.)

Prepare hot roll mix as directed on package adding black pepper and using olive oil instead of butter or margarine. After kneading and resting, roll dough into an 18x9-inch rectangle. Brush with olive oil; sprinkle with cheese and meat.

Starting with the 18-inch side, roll up tightly, pinching end to seal it to the roll. Place, seam side down, onto a baking sheet. Shape into a coil; brush with remaining olive oil. Cover and let rise 20 minutes.

With a sharp knife or kitchen shears cut several Xs into top of coil. Bake in a 375° oven for 30 to 35 minutes. Cool at least 15 minutes before slicing and serving.

MAKES 1 LOAF.

CHILI ANCHO
Wrinkled and dark red-brown, these dried Pablanos can be mild or hot. Can substitute 2 to 3 tsp. paprika for color and taste.

Oat Hot Cakes

1 cup old-fashioned oatmeal
½ cup currants, raisins, dried
  blueberries, cherries or cranberries
1½ cups milk, divided
2 eggs

¼ cup melted butter or margarine
½ cup all-purpose flour
1 Tbsp. sugar
2 tsp. baking powder
½ tsp. salt

Put oatmeal and dried fruit in a bowl; pour over 1 cup milk. Cover and refrigerate overnight.

Beat eggs well, add to oatmeal mixture with ½ cup milk and butter. Beat to blend. Combine flour, sugar, baking powder and salt; add to oatmeal and mix well. Using a salt bag, lightly oil a hot griddle.

Use ¼ cup batter for each pancake. Cook until bubbles form and break on top and edges lose their wet look. Turn and brown second side, about 1 minute for each side.

MAKES 12 TO 15 HOT CAKES.

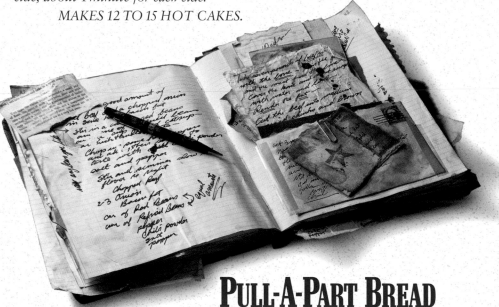

White Grape Apple Butter

1 dozen apples
6 cups white grape or
  apple juice
2 cups sugar
1 Tbsp. ground cinnamon
½ tsp. ground allspice
¼ tsp. ground cloves
1½ tsp. ground nutmeg

Wash and quarter apples removing blossom end, no need to pare or core.

In a large kettle, cook apples in juice until soft, about 45 minutes. Cool and press through a sieve or food mill. There should be 4 to 5 cups apple pulp. Add sugar and spices. Cook slowly, stirring often to prevent sticking, for 1 hour or until thick.

Pack into sterilized jars, adjust lids and process in hot water bath for 10 minutes.

MAKES ABOUT 3 PINTS.

Pull-A-Part Bread

1 recipe Hot Cinnamon Bun dough
  (see page 8)
1½ cups sugar
3 Tbsp. chili powder, optional
2 tsp. cinnamon

2 tsp. ground coriander
½ tsp. ground cloves
½ tsp. ground allspice
½ tsp. ground cardamom
½ to ¾ cup melted butter or margarine

Follow directions for making Hot Cinnamon Bun dough. After dough has risen and been punched down, shape into 30 balls. Combine sugar and spices in a small bowl.

Roll each dough ball in melted butter and then in sugar mixture. Arrange in well-greased 9 or 10-inch tube pan or two 8-inch loaf pans. Sprinkle any remaining sugar over top. Let rise until double, about 1 hour. Bake in a 350° oven for 35 to 40 minutes. Cool 15 minutes before turning out.

MAKES 1 RING OR 2 LOAVES.

WHOLE WHEAT NOODLES

2	cups whole wheat flour	2	eggs
1	cup all-purpose flour	2	egg yolks
1	tsp. salt	5 to 6	Tbsp. water
		4	tsp. vegetable oil

Combine flours and salt in a mixing bowl. Make a well in the middle and add eggs, egg yolks, 3 Tbsp. water and oil; mix with fingers, adding more water as needed to make a stiff dough. Knead to make a smooth dough.

Divide into 3 parts and on a lightly floured surface roll each part into a rectangle, about 12x24 inches. Roll very thin. Let dry for 30 minutes. Roll or fold and slice into ¼ to ½-inch strips. Unroll and dry 30 minutes before cooking.

Drop noodles into a large pot of boiling salted water, cook uncovered until done, 8 to 10 minutes.

MAKES ABOUT 1 POUND.

Note: May be made with 3 cups all-purpose flour only.

NOODLES WITH RED PEPPER SAUCE

3	Tbsp. vegetable oil	3	roasted red peppers (or one 12-ounce jar)
1	medium onion, chopped	½	tsp. cayenne
2	bay leaves	½	tsp. salt
¼	tsp. ground coriander	¼	tsp. ground pepper
⅛	tsp. ground cloves	1	recipe Whole Wheat Noodles, cooked and drained
2	Tbsp. chopped cilantro		
2	cloves garlic, minced		Grated Parmesan or Romano cheese
½	cup water		

Heat oil in saucepan; add onion, bay leaves, coriander, cloves, cilantro and garlic. Cook and stir until onion is tender, 4 to 5 minutes. Add water and simmer for 10 minutes. Remove bay leaves and discard.

Put onion mixture and roasted peppers in food processor or blender and purée. Season with cayenne, salt and pepper, adding water if mixture is too thick.

Heat and serve over hot cooked noodles.

MAKES 4 TO 6 SERVINGS.

Note: May be topped with grated cheese.

Vanilla Cream Sauce

3	Tbsp. sugar	1	egg yolk, beaten
1	Tbsp. cornstarch	1	tsp. vanilla
1	cup milk	½	cup heavy cream

Combine sugar and cornstarch in a saucepan; add milk. Cook and stir over medium heat until mixture thickens. Beat a small amount into egg yolk; stir into hot mixture; cook and stir 1 minute. Add vanilla; chill.

Whip cream and fold into cooled pudding.

WILD BERRY BUCKLE

1½ cups all-purpose flour
1½ Tbsp. sugar
¼ lb. chilled butter or margarine, cubed

5 Tbsp. cold soda water
5 to 6 cups berries (blueberries,
   raspberries, gooseberries, etc.)

½ to ¾ cup sugar
4 Tbsp. butter
2 Tbsp. bourbon

Put flour and 1½ Tbsp. sugar in food processor; add chilled butter and process until mixture becomes crumbly. With processor running, slowly pour in soda water, mixing until mixture forms a ball.

If mixing by hand, cut butter into flour and sugar; slowly add soda water, mixing with a fork.

Press dough mixture into a 4-inch circle; wrap in plastic wrap and refrigerate at least 1 hour.

On a floured surface, pastry cloth, waxed paper or plastic wrap, roll out to fit a 9-inch round or 11x7-inch baking dish allowing a 2-inch overhang. Pour berries into crust; sprinkle sugar over fruit, dot with butter. Drizzle bourbon over fruit. Fold edges of crust over fruit, leaving center open. Sprinkle with additional sugar, if desired.

Bake in a 425° oven for 45 minutes. Serve at room temperature with Vanilla Cream Sauce.

MAKES 6 TO 8 SERVINGS.

High Country Camps

CRUSTY CORN TROUT

4 cleaned and boned
   rainbow or brook trout
⅓ cup all-purpose flour
1 egg
1 Tbsp. water
1 cup yellow cornmeal
¼ cup ground nuts (peanuts,
   pine nuts, walnuts, etc.)
1 tsp. salt
¼ tsp. cracked pepper
¼ tsp. paprika
¼ tsp. ground cumin
Vegetable oil

*Roll trout in flour.
Beat egg with water. Mix
cornmeal, ground nuts, salt,
pepper, paprika and cumin.*

*Dip floured trout into
egg and then into cornmeal.*

*Heat about 1-inch oil in
fry pan over coals or medium
heat. Cook trout, turning
once, until both sides are
brown, 5 minutes per side.
Fish flakes when done.*

MAKES 4 SERVINGS.

*Note: Carry the cornmeal
mixture and flour in paper
bags. Toss in the trout,
shake, and it's ready to fry.*

TOMATO CAN CHILI

¼	cup Italian salad dressing with garlic, well shaken	1	28-ounce can crushed tomatoes	2	4-ounce cans diced chilies
		1	10½-ounce can onion soup with beef stock	2	Tbsp. chili powder
1	lb. ground beef	1	soup can water	1	can pitted black olives (6-ounce dry weight), drained

Heat Italian dressing in a large fry pan or chili pot. Add beef and cook until all pink is gone.

Add cans (tomatoes, onion soup, water and chilies) and chili powder. Bring to a boil and simmer for 30 minutes. Cut drained olives into quarters; add to chili and simmer 5 minutes.

MAKES 6 TO 8 SERVINGS.

Note: One 15-ounce can kidney beans, drained, may be used in place of olives.

HIGH COUNTRY LOAVES

1 recipe Nut and Seed
  Sticks dough
  (see page 23)
Cornmeal

*After dough has
risen and been punched
down, shape into 2
round loaves. Place on
baking sheet that has
been greased and
sprinkled with corn-
meal. Let rest 5 minutes.*

*Place in a cold
oven. Put a pan of boil-
ing water on rack under
loaves. Set oven
temperature to 400°.
Bake 35 to 40 minutes.
When bread is done it
will sound hollow
when tapped.*

MAKES 2 LOAVES.

Porcupine Beef

1 lb. ground beef
½ cup uncooked instant rice
2 eggs, beaten
1 1½-ounce envelope dry
  onion or vegetable soup mix
¼ cup finely chopped sweet
  green or Jalapeño pepper
1 14½-ounce can stewed
  tomatoes
1 12-ounce can or bottle
  of light beer
2 tsp. chili powder
3 Tbsp. flour

Mix together the ground beef, rice, eggs, dry soup mix and chopped pepper. Shape into 6 large balls.

Combine tomatoes, beer and chili powder in a large skillet or 3-quart baker. Heat to boiling over medium heat or in a 350° oven.

Carefully drop meatballs into hot tomato mixture; cover and simmer or bake for 45 to 55 minutes. Lift out meatballs and thicken sauce with 3 Tbsp. flour mixed with cold water, if desired. Serve in deep bowls with cornbread or crusty bread.

MAKES 6 SERVINGS.

Skillet Potatoes

¼ cup bacon fat or vegetable
  oil, divided
4 cups thinly sliced raw
  potatoes (no need to pare)
1 medium onion, thinly sliced

1 tsp. salt
⅛ tsp. cracked pepper
½ tsp. rubbed dried sage
1 tsp. dried parsley flakes,
  optional

Heat half the bacon fat in a heavy skillet over low-medium heat; add potatoes and onion. Sprinkle over part of the seasonings; cover pan and cook about 15 minutes.

Lift and turn potatoes, sprinkling with remaining seasonings. Cover and cook 15 minutes more or until done. Turn or stir potatoes once or twice during last 10 minutes so they cook evenly. Add bacon fat or oil as needed.

MAKES 6 SERVINGS.

CHEESE AND MOLASSES BEANS

¼ lb. sliced smoked bacon
1 onion, chopped
2 cloves garlic, minced
2 28-ounce cans pork and beans
¼ to ½ cup brown sugar, packed
¼ cup molasses
1 Tbsp. steak sauce
½ lb. soft process cheese, cubed

Fry bacon in large skillet.
Pour off fat, return 3 to 4 Tbsp. to
skillet. Fry onion and garlic until
tender. Add pork and beans, brown
sugar to taste, molasses and steak sauce; stir to mix.
Simmer 30 to 35 minutes. Crumble bacon;
add cheese to beans before serving.

MAKES 8 TO 10 SERVINGS.

Note: Mix sugar, molasses and steak sauce
to travel. Soft cheese melts faster.

SAUTÉED CABBAGE

4 cups shredded green cabbage	2 Tbsp. catsup	1 bay leaf
2 Tbsp. butter or margarine	1 small onion or thick slice, studded with	1 apple, cored and sliced
2 to 4 Tbsp. water	2 to 3 cloves	Salt and pepper

Put cabbage in skillet with 2 Tbsp. each, butter, water and
catsup; add onion and bay leaf. Cover and simmer 10 minutes.
Add sliced apple, adding water if needed, and cook 5 minutes.
Discard onion, cloves and bay leaf. Season with salt and pepper.

MAKES 4 TO 5 SERVINGS.

Note: Cabbage, onions and apples travel well for trail cooking.

Whiskey Steak

2 1-inch rib-eye or tenderloin steaks	1 small red onion, sliced	½ tsp. grated orange peel
2 Tbsp. butter or margarine	1 Tbsp. Worcestershire sauce	Salt and pepper
3 Tbsp. orange juice	1 Tbsp. Dijon-style mustard	2 to 3 Tbsp. whiskey

Flatten steaks with heel of hand or a heavy spatula. (Do not pound with a tenderizing mallet.)

Heat butter in a medium skillet; brown meat quickly on both sides. Remove and keep warm. Add orange juice, onion, Worcestershire, mustard and peel to pan; cook and stir until blended.

Return steaks to pan and cook 2 minutes on each side. Remove steaks. Add whiskey to pan; heat and spoon over steaks. Serve immediately.

MAKES 2 SERVINGS.

CHERRY COBBLER

1   1 lb. 5-ounce can cherry
    pie filling
½   cup raisins or dried
    cherries
1   tsp. grated orange
    peel, optional
1   cup all-purpose flour
1½ tsp. baking powder
¼   cup brown sugar,
    packed
½   tsp. cinnamon
¼   cup butter or margarine
½   cup chopped pecans
1   egg, lightly beaten
¼   cup milk

*Combine cherry pie filling, raisins and orange peel in a deep
10-inch fry pan or baking pan; heat to boiling.*

*Mix flour, baking powder, brown sugar and cinnamon together
in a mixing bowl; cut in butter until crumbly. Stir in pecans.*

*Combine egg and milk; add to flour mixture and mix to moisten
dry ingredients. Drop spoonfuls of dough onto hot cherry filling.*

*Bake in covered Dutch oven or deep fry pan over coals or in a
400° oven for 25 to 30 minutes.*

MAKES 6 TO 8 SERVINGS.

*Note: Make dry mixture at cookhouse.
Mix egg and milk together, freeze in a small
plastic container; use when needed.*

HIGH CAMP COOKIES

1 cup butter or margarine
¾ cup brown sugar, packed
¾ cup sugar
1 egg
2 Tbsp. molasses
3 cups all-purpose flour
2 tsp. baking soda
2 tsp. ground black pepper
1 tsp. ground cinnamon

Cream together the butter and sugars until smooth and fluffy. Beat in the egg and molasses.

Combine flour, soda, pepper and cinnamon. Add to first mixture and mix thoroughly.

Divide into 4 parts and shape into 1-inch thick patties. Wrap each in plastic wrap or wax paper; refrigerate about 30 minutes.

Working quickly, roll one part of chilled dough at a time to ⅛-inch thick. Roll between 2 pieces of plastic wrap or wax paper for easier handling. Cut into desired shapes.

If dough softens and is difficult to move, leave it on wax paper and place it on a baking sheet and refrigerate until firm. Remove waxed paper and place cookies on ungreased baking sheet.

Bake in a 400° oven for 7 to 10 minutes. Repeat with remaining chilled dough. Return scraps to refrigerator, chill and reroll.

MAKES ABOUT
4 DOZEN COOKIES.

BREAKFAST BARS

½ cup butter or margarine
1¼ cups brown sugar, packed
2 eggs
⅓ cup molasses
1¾ cups all-purpose flour
1 tsp. baking soda
1 tsp. salt

1 tsp. ground cinnamon
2 cups oatmeal
½ cup chopped walnuts
1 cup raisins, dried cherries or cranberries
1 cup semi-sweet chocolate pieces or chunks

Combine butter, sugar, eggs and molasses in a large mixing bowl. Stir together flour, soda, salt and cinnamon; add to first mixture and stir to mix well.

Stir in oatmeal, walnuts, raisins and chocolate pieces. Spoon into a greased 13x9-inch baking pan and bake in a 400° oven for 12 to 15 minutes or until done. Cut into bars to serve.
MAKES 2 TO 3 DOZEN BARS.

Chuckwagon Roundup

FRESH SOURDOUGH BISCUITS

2 cups all-purpose flour
1 Tbsp. sugar
1 Tbsp. baking powder
¾ tsp. salt
2 cups Sourdough Starter (see below)
2 or 3 Tbsp. shortening

Combine flour, sugar, baking powder and salt in a large bowl; add starter; mix to make firm dough. Add water if needed. Cover and let rest 5 minutes.

Grease a 12-inch Dutch oven or deep iron skillet generously with shortening. Dip fingers into shortening; pinch off dough balls the size of large walnuts and shape them into round balls.

Place close to each other in greased pan; let rise in a warm place for 15 minutes.

Bake over coals in a covered Dutch oven or in a 400° oven for 25 to 30 minutes.

MAKES ABOUT 2 DOZEN.

Sourdough Starter: Soften 1 package active dry yeast in 1-quart lukewarm water in a large crock or bowl. Add 2 Tbsp. sugar and 4 cups all-purpose flour. Beat to mix. Cover with a kitchen towel and place in a warm place to sour for 2 to 4 days. After mixture has reached desired sourness, keep in refrigerator.

Sourdough Cornbread

1 cup yellow cornmeal	1 cup Sourdough
½ cup all-purpose flour	Starter (see page 95)
2 Tbsp. sugar	½ cup buttermilk
2 tsp. baking soda	2 eggs, beaten
½ tsp. salt	2 Tbsp. minced
6 to 8 slices smoked bacon	onion, optional

Combine cornmeal, flour, sugar, soda and salt in a mixing bowl. Fry bacon until crisp, drain on paper towels; reserve ¼ cup drippings. Crumble cooked bacon, set aside.

Combine Sourdough Starter, buttermilk, eggs and reserved bacon fat; add to dry ingredients and beat until well mixed. Stir in onion and crumbled bacon. Pour into a greased 8x8x2-inch baking pan.

Bake in a 350° oven for 25 to 30 minutes.

MAKES 9 SERVINGS.

Dried Apple Cakes

1½ cups chopped dried apples	1 tsp. salt
½ cup dried blueberries	⅓ cup shortening
4 cups water	1 cup buttermilk
1 cup sugar, divided	½ cup brown sugar, packed
2 cups all-purpose flour	1 tsp. ground cinnamon
2 tsp. baking powder	½ tsp. ground nutmeg
1 tsp. baking soda	¼ cup butter or margarine

Cook dried fruit in water until tender. Drain and save 2 cups juice (add water if needed).

Mix ¼ cup sugar with flour, baking powder, baking soda and salt; cut in shortening. Stir in buttermilk. Turn onto floured surface; knead lightly. Pat or roll into a 12x8-inch rectangle.

Sprinkle fruit over dough. Roll from 12-inch side; cut into 12 slices. Put 2 cups juice, remaining sugar, brown sugar, cinnamon, nutmeg and butter into a large oven-going skillet. Bring to a boil.

Lower apple slices into syrup. Bake in a 375° oven for 35 to 40 minutes.

MAKES 12 SERVINGS.

Note: Other dried fruits may be used.

ROASTED CORN RELISH

2 ears corn	1 tsp. chopped, fresh
2 Pablano chili peppers	marjoram
1 medium onion, cut in half	⅓ to ½ cup Green Salsa
1 sweet red pepper	(see page 39)
2 Tbsp. olive oil	Salt

Put corn, peppers and cut onion on an oiled baking sheet; brush vegetables with olive oil. Bake in a 450° oven for 15 to 20 minutes turning once, until lightly browned.

Place peppers in a paper bag to cool. When cool enough to handle, cut corn kernels from cob and chop onion. Peel peppers, removing and discarding stems, seeds and membrane; chop. Combine vegetables, marjoram and salsa. Add salt to taste.

MAKES ABOUT 2 CUPS.

PLUM CRUMBLE

4 cups pitted plums, thinly sliced	¾ tsp. cinnamon
	¼ tsp. salt
⅓ cup brown sugar, packed	1 egg, beaten
½ cup all-purpose flour	½ cup melted butter
½ cup oatmeal	or margarine

Mix sliced plums and brown sugar in the bottom of an 11x7-inch baking pan.

Combine flour, oatmeal, cinnamon and salt in a mixing bowl; add beaten egg and mix until crumbly. Sprinkle evenly over sliced fruit. Pour melted butter over crumbs. Bake in a 375° oven for 40 to 45 minutes.

MAKES 6 TO 8 SERVINGS.

BEER MUFFINS

3 cups all-purpose flour	½ tsp. baking soda
1 Tbsp. baking powder	2 eggs, beaten
1 Tbsp. sugar	⅓ cup vegetable oil
1 tsp. salt	1 12-ounce can beer

Combine flour, baking powder, sugar, salt and soda in a mixing bowl. Add eggs, oil and beer; stir to mix but do not beat.

Spoon into well greased 2¼-inch muffin tin. Bake in a 350° oven for 25 to 30 minutes.

MAKES 12 MUFFINS.

SOURDOUGH FLAPJACKS

1 cup Sourdough Starter (see page 95)
2 cups lukewarm water
2½ cups all-purpose flour
2 eggs, well beaten
2 Tbsp. sugar
⅓ cup half-and-half or buttermilk
2 Tbsp. vegetable oil
1 tsp. baking soda

Mix starter, water and flour together in a mixing bowl; cover and let stand in a warm place overnight.

Stir in eggs, sugar, cream, oil and soda. Let mixture stand for 10 minutes.

Bake on a hot griddle, using ¼ cup batter for each flapjack. Serve with warm maple syrup.

MAKES ABOUT 2 DOZEN 5-INCH FLAPJACKS.

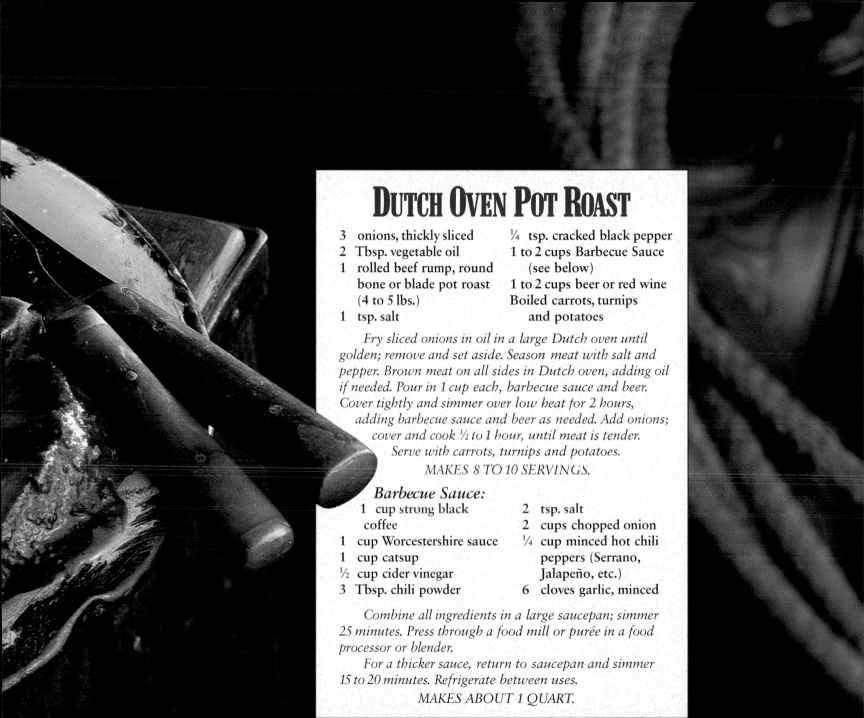

DUTCH OVEN POT ROAST

3 onions, thickly sliced
2 Tbsp. vegetable oil
1 rolled beef rump, round
  bone or blade pot roast
  (4 to 5 lbs.)
1 tsp. salt

¼ tsp. cracked black pepper
1 to 2 cups Barbecue Sauce
  (see below)
1 to 2 cups beer or red wine
Boiled carrots, turnips
  and potatoes

Fry sliced onions in oil in a large Dutch oven until golden; remove and set aside. Season meat with salt and pepper. Brown meat on all sides in Dutch oven, adding oil if needed. Pour in 1 cup each, barbecue sauce and beer. Cover tightly and simmer over low heat for 2 hours, adding barbecue sauce and beer as needed. Add onions; cover and cook ½ to 1 hour, until meat is tender.

Serve with carrots, turnips and potatoes.

MAKES 8 TO 10 SERVINGS.

Barbecue Sauce:

1 cup strong black
  coffee
1 cup Worcestershire sauce
1 cup catsup
½ cup cider vinegar
3 Tbsp. chili powder

2 tsp. salt
2 cups chopped onion
¼ cup minced hot chili
  peppers (Serrano,
  Jalapeño, etc.)
6 cloves garlic, minced

Combine all ingredients in a large saucepan; simmer 25 minutes. Press through a food mill or purée in a food processor or blender.

For a thicker sauce, return to saucepan and simmer 15 to 20 minutes. Refrigerate between uses.

MAKES ABOUT 1 QUART.

ONE PAN CAKE

2½ cups all-purpose flour
1½ cups sugar
½ cup cocoa
2 tsp. baking soda
½ tsp. salt
⅔ cup vegetable oil
2 Tbsp. cider vinegar
1 Tbsp. vanilla
2 cups cold coffee
   or water
⅓ cup sugar
½ tsp. cinnamon

Stir together flour, 1½ cups sugar, cocoa, soda and salt in an ungreased 12x8-inch baking pan.

Make 3 wells in the mixture; pour oil in one, vinegar in one and vanilla in one.

Pour in coffee and stir all with a fork until well mixed. Spread into an even layer.

Combine ⅓ cup sugar and cinnamon; sprinkle half over batter.

Bake in a 350° oven for 35 to 40 minutes. Sprinkle remaining cinnamon sugar over hot cake. Cool 15 or 20 minutes before cutting.

MAKES 6 TO 8 SERVINGS.

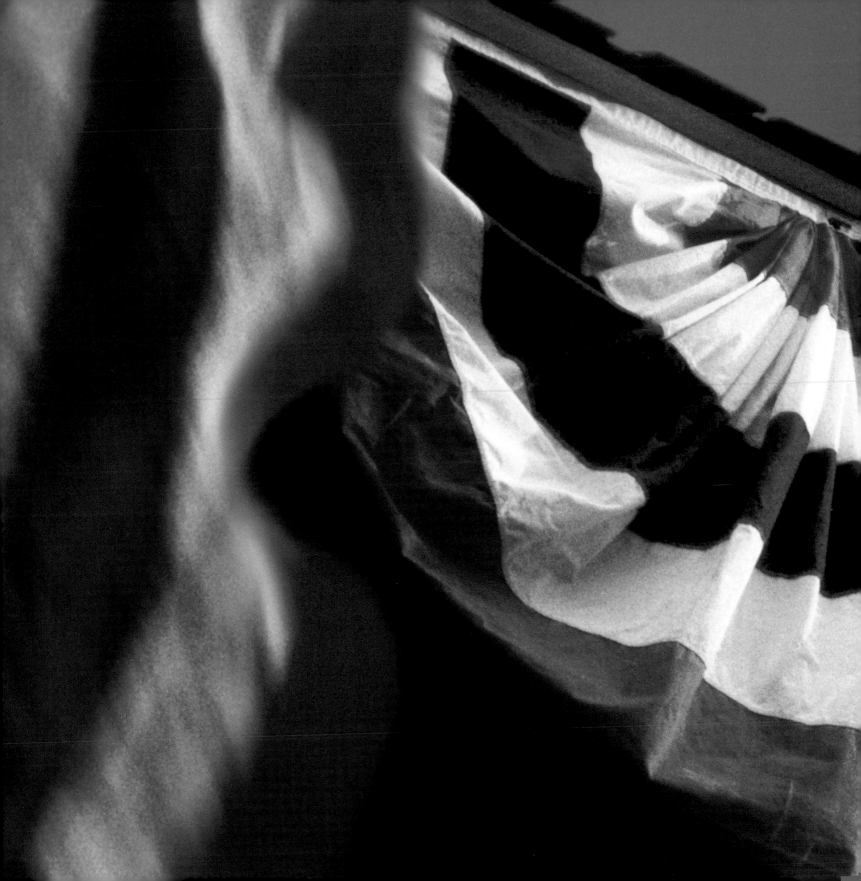

July 4th

SPIT ROASTED GAME BIRDS

2	12-ounce cans beer	2	limes, thinly sliced
½	cup vegetable or olive oil	4	Tbsp. soy sauce
4	Serrano peppers, seeded and finely chopped	4	tsp. Margarita salt
		4	game hens or squab
4	cloves garlic, crushed	2	pheasants or small chickens
1	tsp. dried pepper flakes	8	quail

Combine beer, oil, peppers, garlic, pepper flakes, lime, soy sauce and salt. Put cleaned, washed and dried birds in 1 or 2 large heavy plastic food bags. Pour in marinade and seal bags. Turn and shake until birds are coated with marinade. Refrigerate several hours or overnight, turning bag occasionally.

Remove birds from marinade and position them on a turning spit. Tie legs and wings close to the body to keep them from overcooking.

Roast in a covered grill over medium-hot coals or in a 350° oven. Small birds will take about 30 minutes; larger birds 1 to 1½ hours. Baste every 5 minutes.

Test doneness by pricking with a fork between thigh and body to see if juices run clear.

MAKES 12 SERVINGS.

Barbecued Beef; see recipe page 108.

FAMILY ROUNDUP POTATO SALAD

6 to 8 medium potatoes
½ cup clear Italian dressing
1   cup chopped celery
1   cup chopped cucumber
½ cup chopped parsley
½ cup chopped sweet red
    and/or green pepper

½ cup chopped green onion
½ cup sliced radishes
½ cup mayonnaise
½ cup sour cream
½ lb. cooked bacon, crumbled
½ cup chopped walnuts,
    toasted

Peel and cook potatoes; chop and put them in a mixing bowl (about 6 cups). While potatoes are still warm, pour over Italian dressing; cool.

Add chopped and sliced vegetables. Combine mayonnaise and sour cream; pour over potatoes and vegetables. Mix well. Chill to blend flavors. Top with crumbled bacon and walnuts just before serving.

MAKES 8 TO 10 SERVINGS.

PEPPER SLAW

6 cups chopped or shredded cabbage	½ cup vegctable oil
2 cups sliced red and/or green peppers	1½ tsp. celery salt
	1 tsp. cracked pepper
1½ cups sliced celery	½ tsp. celery seed
1 cup sliced onion	2 Tbsp. sugar
¾ cup shredded carrots	3 Tbsp. cider vinegar
	1 Tbsp. dry mustard

Toss vegetables together in a large mixing bowl. Combine remaining ingredients; pour over vegetables. Toss to mix. Refrigerate for several hours or overnight to blend flavors.

MAKES 10 TO 12 SERVINGS.

HERB ROASTED CORN

Fresh corn in husks, 1 or 2 ears per person
Water
Salt
Salted butter or margarine
Sprigs of fresh herbs–rosemary, thyme, oregano,
    marjoram, mint, cilantro, etc.

    Put corn into a large kettle or washtub; cover with water. Add 1 Tbsp. salt for each gallon of water. Soak the corn in salted water for 30 minutes.
    Remove corn from water and open husks carefully. Remove silk. Brush corn with butter and sprinkle it with several sprigs of herbs; carefully rewrap husks around corn.
    Cook corn in a covered grill over medium-hot coals for 10 minutes, turning once or twice. Corn may be wrapped in aluminum foil before cooking; add 5 minutes cooking time. Foil-wrapped corn may also be cooked in a 450° oven for 25 to 30 minutes.

BARBECUED BEEF

4 to 5 lbs. rump or blade roast	1 to 2 tsp. cayenne
1 to 2 tsp. salt	½ tsp. garlic powder
1 to 2 tsp. black pepper	1½ to 2 cups Barbecue
1 to 2 tsp. dry mustard	Sauce (see page 99)

    Trim excess fat from roast, if needed. Combine seasonings and rub onto all sides of meat. Wrap in plastic wrap or put in plastic food storage bag; refrigerate 24 hours.
    Cook meat in a covered barbecue grill over low coals, turning to cook evenly until done, 1½ to 2 hours. Meat may be cooked in a 325° oven if desired.
    Let meat rest for 10 to 15 minutes before slicing. Serve with warm Barbecue Sauce. Meat may be served as is or piled onto Burger Buns (see page 40) to make hearty sandwiches.

    MAKES 12 TO 16 SERVINGS.

Deviled Eggs

12 large eggs
½ cup mayonnaise
2 tsp. Dijon-style mustard
2 tsp. sweet pickle juice
1 tsp. Worcestershire sauce
½ tsp. salt
¼ tsp. paprika
Dash to ⅛ tsp. cayenne
   or curry powder,
   optional

Cook eggs in simmering water for 20 minutes. Cool under running water.

Peel and then cut eggs in half lengthwise. Remove yolks; set whites aside.

Put still warm yolks into a plastic food storage bag with mayonnaise, mustard, pickle juice, Worcestershire and seasonings; squeeze bag to mash yolks and mix in other ingredients.

Refrigerate filling and egg whites separately. Fill egg whites just before serving. Cut off one corner of bag and press filling into cooked egg whites.

Sprinkle finished eggs with paprika, if desired.

MAKES 12 SERVINGS.

Layered Salad

1 head iceberg lettuce,
   sliced or torn
2 cucumbers or zucchini,
   sliced or chopped
1 medium red and/or green
   pepper, seeded and chopped
3 ripe tomatoes, seeded and
   chopped
1 medium red onion,
   quartered and sliced
2 cups cooked fresh or canned
   corn kernels, drained
2 cups coarsely crushed pretzels
4 hard-cooked eggs, shelled
   and sliced
2 cups mayonnaise
   or
1 cup mayonnaise and
   1 cup sour cream
1 to 2 Tbsp. lemon juice
   (omit if using sour cream)
¼ cup chopped roasted
   red pepper, optional
1½ cups shredded cheddar cheese
2 cups Western Caviar
   (see page 149)

Fill bottom of a large, wide-mouth jar or serving bowl with lettuce. Layer vegetables and crushed pretzels to make a colorful display.

Arrange sliced hard-cooked eggs on top of vegetables.

Mix mayonnaise with lemon juice (or sour cream) and chopped roasted red pepper; spread over egg slices and sprinkle cheese around the edge. Spoon Western Caviar in center of cheese.

Cover tightly with plastic wrap and refrigerate several hours before serving.

MAKES 15 TO 20 SERVINGS.

SNOWY RANGE ICING

½ cup sugar
¼ cup light corn syrup
2 Tbsp. water
2 egg whites
1 tsp. vanilla

Mix sugar, light corn syrup and water in a small saucepan; bring to a boil. Wash down the pan sides with a brush dipped into water. Boil rapidly until a small amount dropped in cold water forms a firm ball or a candy thermometer registers 242°.

Using an electric mixer, beat egg whites until stiff peaks form. Reduce speed of mixer and pour hot syrup into beaten whites, beating constantly. Add vanilla.

Once all syrup is beaten in, beat at high speed until stiff peaks form.

ENOUGH
FROSTING FOR
RED DEVIL'S FOOD
CAKE.

RED DEVIL'S FOOD CAKE

1⅔ cups all-purpose flour	1 cup buttermilk
¾ cup brown sugar, packed	2 Tbsp. light molasses
¾ cup sugar	½ cup butter or margarine (room temperature)
⅓ cup cocoa	2 eggs
1 tsp. salt	1 Tbsp. red food coloring
1 tsp. baking soda	1 tsp. vanilla

Combine flour, sugars, cocoa, salt and baking soda in the large bowl of an electric mixer. Add remaining ingredients and beat at low speed until flour is mixed in. Scrape down the sides of bowl as needed. Beat at high speed for about 3 minutes, scraping bowl once or twice.

Prepare two 8 or 9-inch round pans with cocoa pancoat (see page 161), covering sides and bottom generously. Pans may be coated with shortening and dusted with flour if desired. Pour batter into pans, spreading evenly. Cake batter may be poured into a 13x9-inch pan.

Bake in a 350° oven. Bake layers 30 to 35 minutes; 13x9-inch cake 35 to 40 minutes. Cool layers 10 minutes and turn out onto racks to cool. Cake in a rectangular pan may be left in the pan. Frost with Snowy Range Icing. Sprinkle with grated chocolate or cocoa, if desired.

MAKES 12 TO 16 SERVINGS.

OLD FASHIONED ICE CREAM

2 cups heavy cream
2 cups half-and-half
¾ cup sugar
4 egg yolks, beaten
2 to 3-inch length vanilla bean and/or 2 tsp. vanilla extract
(Need an ice cream freezer)

Heat cream, half-and-half and sugar in a heavy saucepan, stirring 2 or 3 times until sugar melts and mixture heats.

Beat egg yolks in a small bowl. Pour some of the hot cream into beaten yolks, beating to mix. Add yolks to hot cream. Cook, stirring constantly over medium heat, until mixture thickens slightly, about 8 minutes. Do not boil.

Pour into a clean bowl. Cut vanilla bean open and scrape the seeds into hot mixture, mix in. Cover and chill.

Stir before pouring into ice cream freezer. Follow directions for freezing given by the ice cream freezer manufacturer.

MAKES ABOUT 1 QUART.

Chocolate Ice Cream: Melt together 3 ounces semi-sweet chocolate and 1 ounce unsweetened chocolate. Add to the hot milk before adding egg yolks. Proceed as directed above.

Other Additions: Add 1 cup of any of the following to partially frozen ice cream and continue freezing as directed.
Crushed or broken cream-filled chocolate cookies; Chopped toffee candy bars; Crushed hard peppermint candies; Chopped sweet or semi-sweet chocolate; Chopped toasted almonds.

Blue Ribbon Recipes

TOMATO PRESERVES

5 large ripe red or yellow
  tomatoes (3 lbs.)
4½ cups sugar
1 2½-inch cinnamon stick
2 Tbsp. minced fresh
  ginger root or
  preserved ginger
  or
1 tsp. ground ginger
2 lemons or limes, thinly
  sliced

Peel tomatoes and
remove core. Place in a glass
or plastic bowl; add sugar
and let stand overnight.

Drain juice into a large
heavy cooking pot; add
cinnamon stick and minced
ginger root. Boil rapidly until
it thickens, about 20 minutes.

Cut tomatoes into 6 or 8
wedges; add juice with sliced
lemons, cook until mixture
thickens and clears, 20 to 30
minutes. Discard cinnamon
stick, if desired.

Pack into hot sterilized
jars. Adjust lids. Process in a
hot water bath for 20 minutes.
May be kept in refrigerator.
MAKES 5 HALF PINTS.

CREAM BISCUITS

5 cups all-purpose flour	1 package active
¼ cup sugar	dry yeast
1 Tbsp. baking powder	2 Tbsp. lukewarm
1 tsp. baking soda	water
1 tsp. salt	2 cups heavy cream
½ cup cold butter	2 Tbsp. heavy cream
or margarine	

Mix flour, sugar, baking powder, soda and salt in a mixing bowl. Cut in butter until crumbly.

Dissolve yeast in warm water; add with 2 cups cream to dry mixture and mix well.

Turn out onto a lightly floured surface and knead a few times, adding flour if necessary.

Roll out ½-inch thick and cut with 2½-inch cutter. Place on ungreased baking sheet. Brush biscuit tops with 2 Tbsp. cream and sprinkle with sugar, if desired. Let stand 15 minutes before baking. Bake in a 400° oven for 15 minutes or until lightly browned.
MAKES 2 DOZEN.

DILL PICKLES

Pickling cucumbers	Sugar
Dill heads	Mixed pickling spice
Garlic and chili peppers,	Salt
optional	Cider vinegar

Layer cucumbers and dill heads in a large crock or bowl. Add garlic and/or chili peppers.

For each quart of pickles, measure ¼ to ⅓ cup sugar, 2 tsp. each pickling spice and salt and ¾ cup vinegar, heat to boiling and pour over pickles. Prepare more vinegar mixture if it does not cover cucumbers. Cover and let stand 2 or 3 days.

Pickles may be kept in refrigerator for several weeks or canned. To can; drain pickles, pack in clean jars with dill, garlic and peppers. Heat vinegar and pour over. Adjust lids. Process in a hot water bath for 30 minutes.

Candied Dill Slices: *Drain and slice 1-quart Dill Pickles. Add ½ cup sugar and 1 Tbsp. cider vinegar; store in refrigerator for 3 days before serving.*

3 BERRY JAM

3 cups crushed	2 cups crushed	¼ cup fresh
red raspberries	blackberries	lemon
3 cups blueberries	6 cups sugar	or lime juice

Combine crushed and whole berries in a large cooking pot; stir in sugar and lemon juice.

Bring to a boil and cook rapidly for 20 to 30 minutes, until mixture thickens. Reduce heat and cook, stirring occasionally, until desired consistency.

Pour into sterilized jars, adjust lids. Process in a hot water bath for 10 minutes.
MAKES 8 HALF PINTS.

Pickled Beets

8 to 12 medium beets
1 cup sugar
¾ tsp. salt
6 whole allspice
6 whole cloves
1 2½-inch cinnamon stick
1¾ cups vinegar
¾ cup water
1 onion, sliced

Cook beets until tender, about 30 to 40 minutes. Cool under running water. Peel and slice about 6 cups. Set aside. Combine sugar, salt, spices, vinegar and water; simmer 15 minutes.

Add beets and onion; simmer 5 minutes.

Pack into jars; adjust caps. Process in hot water bath for 30 minutes.

MAKES 3 PINTS.

Herb Vinegars

Large bunches fresh herbs (dill, basil, oregano, thyme, chives with blossoms, mint, rosemary)
4 cups red or white wine or cider vinegar

Black, red or white peppercorns, dill, mustard or celery seed
Garlic
Red or green chili peppers
Lemons

Wash and dry enough herbs to fill a quart jar; press down with a wooden spoon to crush stems and release flavor. Fill jar with vinegar. Cover and let stand 2 days.

Strain vinegar and discard herbs. Fill jars loosely with fresh herbs. (Use one herb or in combination.) Use any or all remaining ingredients. Pour in strained vinegar and let stand in a sunny window for 2 weeks.

Strain again. Fill jars with a colorful combination of fresh herbs and other ingredients; pour in strained vinegar.

MAKES 1 QUART.

Sweet Sour Carrots

1 16-ounce bag small carrots or
4 cups ½-inch sliced carrots
¾ cup sugar
¾ cup cider or flavored vinegar

2 tsp. mustard seed
1 tsp. celery seed
1 1½-inch cinnamon stick, broken in half
3 whole cloves
1 bay leaf

Cook carrots in salted water for 5 to 7 minutes, until tender crisp. Drain, reserving ¾ cup of cooking water.

Combine reserved water, sugar, vinegar, mustard seed, celery seed, cinnamon, cloves and bay leaf in a saucepan. Bring to a boil and simmer 10 minutes; add carrots and bring to a boil.

Pack into hot sterilized jars. Adjust lids. Process in a hot water bath for 30 minutes.

MAKES 2 PINTS.

Farmer's Market Chili Sauce

8 large ripe tomatoes
2 large apples
2 large ripe pears
2 large sweet red and/or green peppers
2 medium onions
2 to 4 Serrano chili peppers

1 large clove garlic, minced
1½ cups cider vinegar
1 cup sugar
2 tsp. salt
2 2½-inch cinnamon sticks
½ tsp. whole cloves

Peel, seed and core tomatoes; pare and core apples and pears. Seed red peppers. Chop tomatoes, apples, pears, red peppers and onions; put into a large cooking pot.

Seed and mince chili peppers; mince garlic. Add to tomatoes with remaining ingredients. Simmer, stirring occasionally, until mixture thickens. Pack in jars; adjust lids and process in hot water bath for 15 minutes.

MAKES 4 PINTS.

APPLE CRUMB PIE

Pastry for 1 pie shell (see page 145)
6 cooking apples
2 tsp. lemon juice
½ cup sugar
1 cup all-purpose flour
1 cup brown sugar, packed
½ tsp. ground cinnamon
½ tsp. ground ginger
¼ tsp. ground mace
½ cup butter or margarine

Prepare pastry as directed.

Pare apples, cut into eighths and remove core. Sprinkle with lemon juice while placing in a mixing bowl. When all apples are prepared, sprinkle with ½ cup sugar, tossing to mix. Arrange apples in unbaked pie shell.

Mix together flour, brown sugar and spices; cut in butter until crumbly. Spoon evenly over apples.

Bake in a 400° oven for 40 to 45 minutes.

MAKES 6 TO 8 SERVINGS.

STRAWBERRY PIE

Pastry for 1 pie shell (see page 145)
3 ounces cream cheese, softened
2 Tbsp. milk
1 Tbsp. sugar
1 10-ounce package frozen strawberries, defrosted
½ cup sugar
3 Tbsp. cornstarch
¼ cup strawberry jelly
1 quart fresh strawberries
Mallow Whipped Cream, optional (see below)

Prepare pastry as directed.

Beat together cream cheese, milk and 1 Tbsp. sugar; spread in bottom of pie shell. Bake in a 475° oven 8 to 10 minutes. Cool.

Press defrosted strawberries through a sieve to remove seeds. Combine ½ cup sugar and cornstarch in a saucepan; stir in sieved berries and jelly. Cook and stir until mixture thickens.

Arrange fresh strawberries in baked crust, cutting large berries in half. Spoon over strawberry glaze; chill. Top with Mallow Whipped Cream.

MAKES 6 TO 8 SERVINGS.

***Mallow Whipped Cream:** Heat ¼ cup milk. Stir in 2 cups miniature marshmallows. Cool. Fold in 1 cup whipped cream.*

BERRY CHERRY PIE

Pastry for double crust pie (see page 145)
3 cups pitted fresh or frozen tart red cherries
1½ to 2 cups fresh or frozen raspberries, blackberries or blueberries
1 3-ounce package tapioca pudding mix
½ cup sugar
3 Tbsp. butter or margarine
Cream, optional
Sugar, optional

Prepare pastry as directed. Combine cherries, berries, pudding mix and sugar; pour into pre-pared bottom crust and dot top with butter.

Top with second crust. Pinch and crimp edge as desired. Slash top crust to vent. If desired, brush with cream and sprinkle with sugar before baking.

Bake in a 400° oven for 50 to 55 minutes or until crust browns and filling boils. Allow 10 minutes more if using frozen fruit.

MAKES 6 TO 8 SERVINGS.

PECAN PEACH PIE

Pastry for 1 pie shell   ¾   cup light brown
   (see page 145)   sugar, packed
1   21-ounce can peach pie filling   2   egg yolks, beaten
1   cup sour cream or half-and-half   1   cup pecan halves

Prepare pastry as directed.

Spread peach pie filling in unbaked pie shell. Combine sour cream, brown sugar and egg yolks, stirring to mix. Add pecans. Pour over peach filling.

Bake in a 450° oven for 10 minutes; reduce oven temperature to 350° and bake 30 to 40 minutes or until custard is set. Cool.

MAKES 8 SERVINGS.

Note: One 29-ounce can sliced peaches may be used. Drain and save juice. In a saucepan, mix juice with 2 Tbsp. quick-cooking tapioca. Cook and stir until thickened. Add peaches; cool before filling pie shell.

RHUBARB PIE

Pastry for double crust pie   1½ cups sugar
   (see page 145)   1   tsp. grated orange peel
4   cups diced fresh or   ¼   tsp. ground mace
   defrosted frozen rhubarb   1 to 2 Tbsp. butter
¼   cup all-purpose flour   or margarine

Prepare pastry as directed.

Toss rhubarb with flour, sugar, orange peel and mace. Pour into prepared bottom crust; dot with bits of butter.

Top fruit with lattice or plain crust. Pinch and crimp edge; slash top crust to vent.

Bake in a 450° oven for 10 minutes; reduce oven heat to 350° and bake 40 to 45 minutes. Serve at room temperature.

MAKES 6 TO 8 SERVINGS.

Note: 2 cups fresh strawberries may replace 2 cups rhubarb.

FIRST PRIZE

WHITE
SANDS
COUNTY
...R

STEAK ON A GRILL

⅓ cup black or mixed peppercorns
1 tsp. coriander seeds
2 Tbsp. coffee beans
1 tsp. salt
6 2-inch thick T-bone,
   4 porterhouse or 3 sirloin steaks
1½ cups red wine
¼ cup steak sauce
¼ cup soy sauce
2 cloves garlic, crushed
2 tsp. paprika

Grind pepper, coriander seeds and coffee beans in a spice grinder or pepper mill. Add salt. Press spice mixture onto both sides of steaks, put into large plastic food bags or a glass baking dish.

Combine wine, steak sauce, soy sauce, garlic and paprika; pour over beef. Close bags or cover dish and refrigerate several hours. Turn steak once or twice as it marinates.

Remove meat from marinade, pat dry with paper towels. Reserve marinade.

Cook steaks over medium coals to desired doneness, allowing 7 to 10 minutes per side for rare; 10 to 15 minutes per side for medium. Brush with marinade as they cook.

Let steaks stand a few minutes before slicing. Steaks may be broiled, if desired.

Boil reserved marinade to reduce, adding more wine if desired. Serve with sliced steak.

MAKES 12 TO 18 SERVINGS.

For Barbecue Ribs; see recipe page 126.

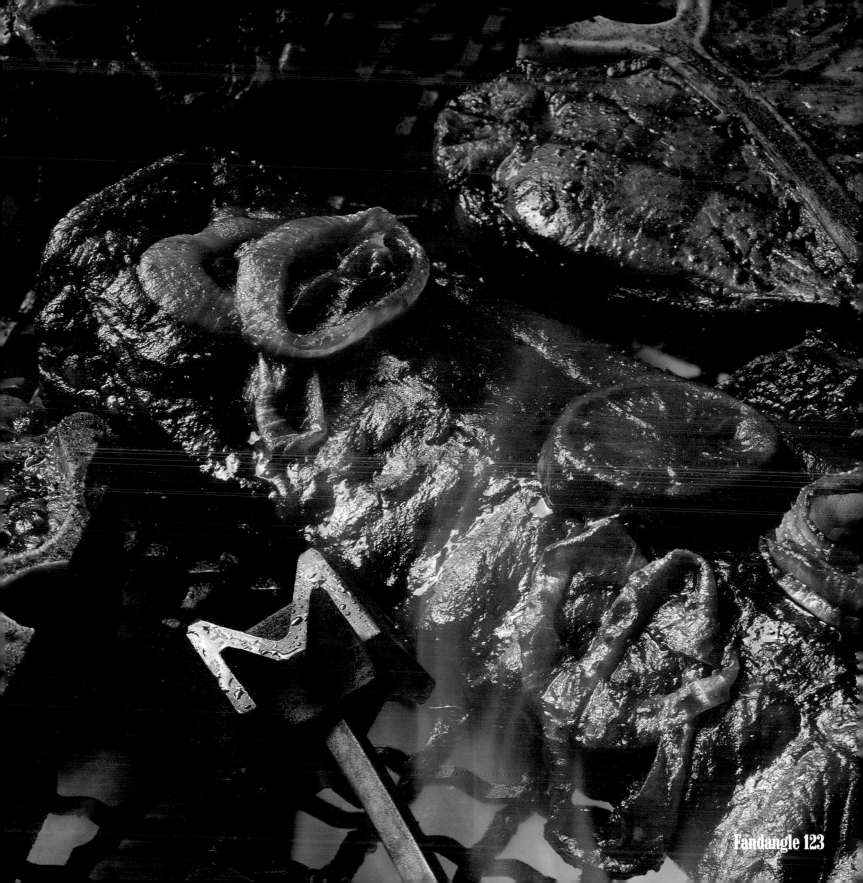

ROASTED VEGETABLES

6 to 9 ripe plum tomatoes
4 Tbsp. minced parsley
2 cloves garlic, minced
Salt and pepper
⅓ to ½ cup olive oil
2 medium zucchini and/or yellow squash
2 large sweet green, yellow and/or red peppers
6 each, new potatoes, bulb onions and small eggplants

Wash tomatoes, remove stem end and cut in half. Arrange in a single layer, cut side up, in a baking dish.

Sprinkle 1½ Tbsp. minced parsley and 1 clove minced garlic over tomatoes. Sprinkle with salt and pepper. Pour 2 or 3 Tbsp. olive oil over tomatoes. Roast in a 425° oven for 45 minutes. Add other vegetables after 20 minutes.

Wash and trim zucchini, cut into thick lengthwise slices, then cut slices in half. Wash peppers; cut into wedges; remove stem and seeds. Wash potatoes, onions and eggplant; cut in half.

Arrange vegetables in a single layer in baking dish with tomatoes; brush with remaining olive oil and sprinkle with parsley, garlic, salt and pepper. Bake for 20 to 25 minutes more until done.

MAKES 6 TO 8 SERVINGS.

SKEWERS OF GARDEN VEGETABLES WITH FIRE POT SAUCE

Small whole vegetables (zucchini, patty pan squash, yellow squash,
  cherry tomatoes, cherry peppers, pea pods, etc.)
Large vegetables cut into chunks or slices (peppers, onions, zucchini,
  eggplant, butternut squash, mushrooms, corn cob slices, etc.)
6   long metal or wooden skewers
Olive oil
Seasoning salt

*Wash and trim vegetables, cutting as needed. Soak wooden skewers
in water before loading. Thread a colorful assortment on skewers. Brush
vegetables with olive oil and sprinkle with seasoning salt. Grill over
medium-hot fire or broil for 2 to 4 minutes, turning to cook all sides.*
MAKES 6 SERVINGS.

Fire Pot Sauce: *Combine 8-ounces Deluxe Process American
or Old English sharp cheese (cut into cubes),
1 cup bottled mild red salsa, 1 or 2 Serrano peppers
(finely chopped) and ½ tsp. Worcestershire sauce
in a small saucepan; heat until cheese melts.
Serve over vegetables.*

Sun Tea & Lemonade

Sun Tea

Place 4 tea bags or 4 tsp. loose tea in a 2-quart glass jar. Add 1½-quarts cold water and cover. Let stand in sun for at least 3 hours or until of desired strength. Remove tea bags or strain into a pitcher filled with ice cubes. Pour into ice-filled glasses.

MAKES ABOUT 12 GLASSES.

Iced Lemon Tea

Pour 4 cups boiling water over 8 tea bags or 8 tsp. loose tea; let stand until of desired strength. Strain and cool to room temperature.

Cut a long strip of peels from 2 lemons, leaving white portion.

Squeeze lemons, straining out seeds, into a large pitcher. Add ⅓ to ½ cup sugar, lemon peel and 1 quart ice cubes; pour over tea. Stir to mix. Pour into ice-filled glasses.

MAKES 8 GLASSES.

Lemonade

Add 3 Tbsp. freshly squeezed lemon juice (seeds removed) and ⅓ to ½ cup sugar to 1 pint water. Sugar and water may be simmered for 2 minutes to dissolve sugar. Mix and pour over ice cubes.

Pink Lemonade

Add 1 Tbsp. grenadine to above recipe.

Sparkling Lemonade

Mix 3 Tbsp. freshly squeezed lemon juice (seeds removed) with ⅓ to ½ cup sugar. Allow to stand a few minutes to soften sugar. Pour into 3 ice-filled glasses; pour in club soda.

MAKES 3 GLASSES.

Lemonade for a Crowd

Boil together 4 cups water and 8 cups sugar; cool. Add 10 cups lemon juice and four 16-ounce cans pineapple juice concentrate. Add 4 gallons water and pour over a block of ice. Float lemon slices.

MAKES ABOUT 100 SERVINGS.

Barbecued Ribs

4   sides lean back ribs or spareribs
1   tsp. salt
½   tsp. freshly cracked pepper
1   large onion, sliced
1   lime, sliced
½   cup strong black coffee
½   cup tomato paste
½   cup honey
2   Tbsp. brown sugar
2   Tbsp. tequila
1   tsp. Worcestershire sauce
¼   tsp. Tabasco® sauce

Trim excess fat from ribs; sprinkle both sides with salt and pepper.

Place, rib side up, on rack in a covered barbecue grill; cook 60 minutes, turning occasionally. Place onions and lime slices on meaty side of ribs for the last 20 minutes.

To make sauce, combine remaining ingredients; brush ribs generously with sauce and continue cooking for 30 minutes or until ribs are tender. Continue to brush ribs with sauce as they cook.

Ribs may be cooked in a 400° oven. Follow same directions as above.

MAKES 4 TO 6 SERVINGS.

See photo page 123.

EGG COFFEE FOR A CROWD

Heat 8 quarts cold water to boiling in a large coffee pot; let water boil 2 minutes.

Put 1 cup ground roast coffee and 1 egg in the center of a square of cheesecloth. Bring up edges like a sack and tie tightly around coffee and egg.

Make 3 more coffee and egg bags. Break eggs in cheesecloth bags and using hands, muddle together with coffee.

Drop sacks of egg-moistened coffee into boiling water. Boil 4 minutes.

Remove coffee bags and discard. Add ½ cup cold water to settle the grounds.

MAKES 32 CUPS OF COFFEE.

TEX-MEX RICE SALAD

1 large red onion	¼ tsp. cayenne	2 cups cut-up jicama
⅓ cup lime juice	⅓ cup olive oil	1 orange, peeled and sectioned
½ tsp. salt	2 cups cooked rice	⅓ cup chopped cilantro

Thinly slice red onion. Combine lime juice, salt, cayenne and olive oil; pour over onion and let stand several hours or overnight.

Combine rice, 2 cups jicama, orange, cilantro in a mixing bowl; add onion mixture. Toss to mix. Let stand to blend flavors.

MAKES 4 TO 6 SERVINGS.

FREE FORM TART

Pastry for 3 pie shells (see page 145)
Apples, plums or pears
¼ cup lemon juice
    2 tsp. sugar
    1 tsp. vanilla
½ cup soft butter or margarine
½ cup sugar

1 egg
2 Tbsp. all-purpose flour
1 cup ground nuts (walnuts, pecans, pine nuts or almonds)
1 cup shredded cheddar or Swiss, or crumbled blue cheese
Sugar, optional

Turn prepared pastry onto a lightly floured surface, roll from the center outward to form a rough 12 to 14-inch circle, oval or other shape. Transfer to a baking sheet or pizza tin. Turn the edges up and in, pinching to form a standing collar. Refrigerate while preparing fruit and cheese mixture.

Combine lemon juice, 2 tsp. sugar and vanilla; set aside.

Cream butter and ½ cup sugar together; add egg and flour; beating until well mixed. Add selected ground nuts and cheese. Try pine nuts and cheddar cheese with apples, almonds and Swiss cheese with plums, walnuts and blue cheese with pears. Set aside.

Prepare selected fruit—wash and core 3 or 4 apples; slice into thin circles, toss with lemon juice mixture and marinate for 20 minutes.

Wash 4 or 5 plums and slice into thin wedges, discard pit. Marinate in lemon juice mixture.

Pare 3 or 4 firm pears and remove core. Cut into thin slices. Marinate in lemon juice mixture.

Take pastry from refrigerator; check edges and rework collar if needed. Spread nut and cheese mixture over crust; arrange fruit on top and sprinkle with sugar, if desired.

Bake in a 400° oven for 40 to 45 minutes or until crust is browned and fruit is cooked. Cool before serving.

MAKES 1 TART, 12 TO 16 SERVINGS.

Rodeo

Fry Bread Tacos

1 recipe Sopaipilla (Fry Bread) dough (see page 37)
Vegetable oil
1 lb. fresh sausage
3 to 4 cups cooked Pinto Beans (see page 31)
3 cups shredded lettuce
1 to 2 cups chopped fresh tomato
1 to 2 cups chopped onion
Green or Red Salsa (see pages 38, 39)
½ to 2 cups shredded Monterey Jack, colby or CoJack cheese

Prepare Sopaipilla dough as directed in recipe. After kneading and resting, divide into 12 portions. Keep dough covered except when rolling out. Roll each portion into a rough 6 or 7-inch circle. Cover and set aside.

When all dough pieces are rolled, heat a skillet or griddle. Skim the pan with about 1 tsp. vegetable oil. Drop 1 dough circle onto hot oil, spinning to coat. Cook until the dough bubbles and puffs, about 1 minute. Turn and cook second side.

Repeat with remaining dough circles, rerolling if needed.

Cook sausage until done; add to beans and heat to boiling.

Spoon beans and sausage on top of fry bread. Top with lettuce, tomato onion and salsa. Sprinkle with cheese.

MAKES 12 SERVINGS.

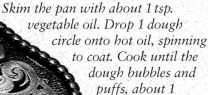

Brisket Boiled in Beer

3 to 4 lbs. beef brisket	1 small cinnamon stick
1 medium onion, sliced	1 tsp. mustard seed
4 cloves garlic, cut in half	2 cans dark beer
3 sprigs fresh thyme	4 to 6 Tbsp. olive oil
1 bay leaf	1½ tsp. salt
6 peppercorns	1 6-ounce can tomato
2 whole allspice	paste

Put meat into a deep bowl or large plastic bag; add onion, garlic, seasonings. Pour beer over all; cover bowl or seal bag; let marinate in refrigerator for 2 days.

Remove meat from marinade and pat dry; reserve marinade. Brown meat in olive oil in a large Dutch oven; sprinkle meat with salt. Add marinade to Dutch oven and heat to boiling.

Cover and simmer until tender, about 2 hours. Lift meat from cooking pan; keep warm. Strain and save marinade, discarding seasonings. Boil strained marinade rapidly until it is reduced by half. Stir in tomato paste, taste and adjust seasonings. Thicken with flour and water if desired. Serve sliced beef with sauce.

MAKES 8 SERVINGS.

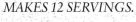

WALKING BEEF SANDWICH

1   6 to 8 inch long sandwich roll
¼ cup cooked Pinto Beans, drained (see page 31)
2 to 4 ounces cooked Barbecue Beef, sliced
   (see page 108)
1 or 2 slices onion
Barbecue Sauce (see page 99)

*Cut roll in half lengthwise, leaving one edge
attached. Open roll and pull out soft center.
Mash beans and spread them on bottom of roll.*

*Layer on sliced beef and onion. Spoon over
Barbecue Sauce. Close sandwich and wrap tightly
in waxed or parchment paper, folding in ends.
Cut in half through both paper and sandwich.*

MAKES 1 SERVING.

SUGAR AND SPICE DONUTS

1½ cups all-purpose flour
1½ cups whole wheat flour

1 tsp. baking soda
1 tsp. baking powder
½ tsp. salt

½ tsp. nutmeg
1 cup buttermilk
1 egg, beaten
⅔ cup sugar

2 Tbsp. melted butter or margarine
Cooking oil
Cinnamon sugar

Combine 2 flours, baking soda, baking powder, salt and nutmeg in a mixing bowl. Beat together buttermilk, egg and sugar; add to the first mixture with melted butter; mix until a soft dough forms. Turn dough out onto a floured surface; knead lightly. Pat and roll dough to ½-inch thick. Cut with a floured cutter. Fry donuts and holes in hot oil (375°) in a deep fat fryer or large saucepan, turning once and frying 3 minutes on each side. Drain on paper towels. While hot, dip in cinnamon sugar.
MAKES 15 DONUTS AND HOLES.

Choco Chunk Cookies

4 ounces unsweetened chocolate	1½ cups all-purpose flour
½ cup butter or margarine	1½ tsp. baking powder
1 cup sugar	1 cup semi-sweet chocolate chunks or chips
¼ tsp. salt	1 cup broken walnuts
3 eggs	½ cup confectioners' sugar
1 Tbsp. vanilla	2 Tbsp. cocoa

Melt unsweetened chocolate and butter together over low heat, cool slightly.

Beat sugar and salt into melted chocolate. Add eggs, one at a time, beating after each addition. Add vanilla and beat until light and creamy, about 5 minutes.

Mix flour and baking powder together; add to chocolate mixture, stirring to mix well. Stir in chocolate chunks and walnuts. Refrigerate 30 minutes.

Mix confectioners' sugar and cocoa together in a small bowl. Shape dough into balls, using a heaping tablespoon. Roll dough balls in sugar-cocoa mixture. Place on a greased baking sheet.

Bake in a 375° oven for about 10 to 12 minutes. Cool 5 minutes before removing from baking sheet.

MAKES ABOUT 2½ DOZEN COOKIES.

Big Cookies

3 eggs, beaten	1½ cups peanut butter
1 cup brown sugar, packed	4½ cups oatmeal
½ cup sugar	1 cup semi-sweet chocolate, chopped or pieces
1 tsp. vanilla	¼ cup chopped dates or raisins
2 tsp. baking soda	¾ cup chopped walnuts
½ cup soft butter or margarine	

Combine eggs, sugars, vanilla, baking soda, butter and peanut butter. Add remaining ingredients and mix thoroughly. Drop by heaping teaspoonfuls onto a greased baking sheet; flatten slightly. Bake in a 350° oven for 12 minutes.

MAKES ABOUT 2 DOZEN BIG COOKIES.

Watermelon Surprise

2 small to medium watermelons	1 to 2 cups Margarita mix Tequila

Wash and dry watermelons. With a long, sharp knife, mark off a 5 to 6-inch circle on top of the watermelons; cut a deep cone into the center of each watermelon. Remove the plug. Turn watermelons over and let them drain for about 30 minutes; discard juice.

Turn melons open side up. Into one pour ½ to 1 cup liquid Margarita mix to fill cavity, wait a bit and add more as it is absorbed. (If using dry Margarita mix, prepare as directed and fill melon.)

For second melon, measure a similar amount of mix and combine with tequila, using 3 parts mix to 1 part tequila. Pour into second watermelon.

Let melons stand as liquid is absorbed. Replace plug. Mark one melon alcoholic and the other melon non-alcoholic.

Thanksgiving

STUFFED PEPPERS

½ cup butter or margarine
½ lb. mushrooms, chopped
1 cup minced parsley
1 cup sliced green onions
1 cup cooked rice
⅔ cup chopped toasted pecans or almonds
1 tsp. ground ginger
¼ cup chicken broth
Salt
8 medium sweet peppers

In a fry pan melt butter; add mushrooms, parsley and green onions. Cook until tender. Add rice, pecans and ginger; stirring to mix. Add chicken broth; cook and stir until liquid is absorbed. Makes 3½ cups stuffing.

Wash and clean peppers. Cut off top and carefully scoop out interior. Blanch peppers in boiling salted water for 3 to 5 minutes. Remove from cooking water and cool under running water. Turn upside down to drain.

Spoon rice stuffing into peppers and replace tops. Arrange them in a baking dish. Cover with aluminum foil. Bake in a 350° oven for 35 to 45 minutes.

MAKES 8 SERVINGS.

CRANBERRY SAUCE

1 12-ounce package cranberries
⅓ cup orange juice or water
1 cup sugar
1 2½-inch cinnamon stick
1 long strip orange peel

Combine all ingredients in a saucepan. Bring to a boil and cook over medium heat for 10 minutes. Cool before serving. Discard cinnamon stick and orange peel.

MAKES ABOUT 2½ CUPS.

MASHED POTATOES AREN'T PLAIN ANYMORE

4 cups mashed potatoes, about 2 lbs.
¼ cup diced lean slab bacon
1 medium onion, cut in half and thinly sliced
1 Tbsp. finely chopped Chipotle peppers
¼ to ½ cup shredded cheddar or
  Parmesan cheese
2 cloves garlic, minced (cook with bacon
  and onion)
1 tsp. chopped fresh rosemary

Prepare mashed potatoes as usual, omitting butter. Fry bacon and onion together until bacon is crisp and onion is browned. Add to potatoes, mixing thoroughly. Check seasonings. Add one or more of the other ingredients, if desired.

MAKES 6 TO 8 SERVINGS.

GOBBLER FRAME SOUP WITH SLIP JACKS

Bones and leftover	2 carrots	3 celery ribs
meat from	2 medium onions,	2 parsley stems
Roast Turkey	stuck with 3 or 4	1 bay leaf
(see page 143)	whole cloves	Water, about 3 quarts

Break up the turkey carcass and put bones into a large soup pot with cleaned carrots, onions, celery, parsley stems and bay leaf; add water to cover. Bring to a boil and simmer for 1 to 1½ hours. Taste and add seasoning as needed. Strain to remove bones.

Lift out vegetables and press them through a food mill or purée; return to soup stock. Pick meat from bones. Chop leftover meat; add to soup. Bring to a boil.

Drop Slip Jacks into boiling soup and cook about 10 minutes.

MAKES 8 TO 10 SERVINGS.

Slip Jacks: *Combine 1 beaten egg, 2 Tbsp. milk and ½ tsp. salt in a mixing bowl. Add about 1 cup flour to make a stiff dough. Cover and let rest for 10 minutes. Turn out onto a floured surface and roll to a 16 x 12-inch rectangle. Cut into 1½-inch squares. Use as directed.*

ROAST TURKEY
WITH JALAPEÑO CORNBREAD

1	16 to 20 lb. roasting turkey	1	cup coarsely chopped pecans
1	recipe Jalapeño Cornbread (see page 23)	1	tsp. salt
1½	cups cubed toasted white bread	1	tsp. ground pepper
⅓ to ½	cup butter or margarine	¼	tsp. cayenne
3	celery ribs, chopped		Turkey or chicken broth
1	medium green pepper, chopped	¼ to ½	cup whiskey or tequila, optional
2	medium onions, chopped		Melted butter or margarine

Wash and dry turkey, removing giblets, neck and excess fat from cavity. Discard fat. Refrigerate turkey while making stuffing.

Crumble cornbread into a large mixing bowl; add cubed toast. Melt butter in a large fry pan; add chopped vegetables and cook until tender. Add pecans; cook and stir until coated with butter. Add seasonings. Add turkey broth until desired moistness. Cool before stuffing bird.

Brush inside of turkey with whiskey, if desired. Spoon stuffing into cavity. Tuck legs under flap or tie with string, pinning if necessary to close opening. Spoon additional stuffing into neck opening; tuck wings under the back. Pin opening shut if needed. Place turkey, breast side up, on a rack in large roasting pan. Brush with whiskey and melted butter.

Bake in a 325° oven for 5½ to 6½ hours. Release the legs for the last 2 hours. Roast until internal temperature reaches 185°. Remove turkey from oven and let stand for 20 minutes before carving.

MAKES 25 TO 30 SERVINGS.

PASTRY

One Pie Shell
1   cup all-purpose flour
½   tsp. salt
⅓   cup cold lard or shortening
2 or 3 Tbsp. chilled club soda, lemon-lime or other flavored soda or ice water

Two Pie Shells or Double Pie Crust
2   cups all-purpose flour
1   tsp. salt
⅔   cup cold lard or shortening
4 or 5 Tbsp. chilled club soda, lemon-lime or other flavored soda or ice water

Combine flour and salt; cut in lard to make a crumbly mixture. Sprinkle with 1 Tbsp. of cold soda, tossing with a fork to mix; repeat until flour is moistened and can be pressed into a ball.

Shape into 1 flat rounded ball if making 1 pie shell; 2 balls for 2 pie shells or 1 double crust pie. Wrap ball in plastic wrap or waxed paper and let rest for 5 minutes.

On a lightly floured surface, roll 1 ball into an 11 to 13-inch circle to fit an 8, 9 or 10-inch pie plate. Fold into quarters or roll around rolling pin and transfer to pie plate.

Follow directions for single crust or double crust pies.

PUMPKIN PIE

Pastry for 1 pie shell
   (see above)
1   16-ounce can pumpkin
¾   cup sour cream
¾   cup milk

¾   cup brown sugar
1½ to 2 tsp. pumpkin pie spice
3   eggs, separated
¼   cup chopped pecans
2   tsp. butter or margarine

Prepare pastry as directed. Set aside.

Combine pumpkin, sour cream and milk, beating until smooth. Add brown sugar, spice and egg yolks; beat until well mixed.

Beat egg whites until stiff peaks form. Stir a small amount of the pumpkin mixture into beaten egg whites to lighten, then fold it into pumpkin.

Pour pumpkin mixture into prepared pie crust. Bake in 375° oven for 50 to 60 minutes or until done.

Toast pecans in butter in a small fry pan, stirring constantly. Cool; sprinkle over pumpkin pie before serving.

MAKES 8 TO 10 SERVINGS.

Christmas

WILD WEST BOWL

2 lemons
2 oranges
2 6-ounce packages mixed dried
   fruit or dried apples
10 whole cardamom pods
12 whole allspice
12 whole cloves
2 4-inch cinnamon sticks
3 quarts apple cider
1 quart citrus juice
2 cups light rum, optional

   Cut peel from lemon and orange
in long strips, set aside. Squeeze juice
from fruit, set aside.
   Put dried fruit, lemon peel and
orange peel into a large cooking pot.
Tie spices in a cheesecloth bag and add
to fruit mixture with apple cider; bring
to a boil. Cover and simmer 20 minutes.
   Add citrus juice (combine juices
from above) and rum; heat to a slow
simmer and remove from heat.
Do not boil.
   Remove spice bag and strain out
fruit, discard or save dried fruit for
Dried Apple Cakes (see page 66).
Serve hot in mugs or cups.
   MAKES 24 (½ CUP) SERVINGS.

WESTERN CAVIAR

2   15-ounce cans
    black beans or
    black-eyed peas
2   cloves garlic, cut up
1   medium onion,
    cut up
½   tsp. salt
1   tsp. pepper
⅓   cup parsley
⅓   cup olive oil
3 to 4 Tbsp. red wine
    vinegar

Rinse and drain beans. Place in a food processor with remaining ingredients. Process with an on and off motion for about 1 minute. Refrigerate overnight to allow flavors to blend. Serve with chips, crackers or toast.

MAKES 3 CUPS.

WILD MUSHROOM SOUP

1   package (1 to 2 oz.) dried mushrooms
    (porcinis, chanterelles, morels, shiitake, etc.)
½   cup warm water
2   Tbsp. butter or margarine
2   Tbsp. olive oil
1   cup finely chopped onion
3   cloves garlic, minced
2 to 3 cups chopped fresh wild mushrooms
    (Portobellos, porcini, morels, shiitake, etc.)
½   lb. cultivated white mushrooms, sliced
2   large ripe tomatoes
1   tsp. salt
¼   tsp. ground pepper
¼   cup chopped parsley
1   tsp. dried marjoram
1   tsp. dried thyme
6   cups beef broth or stock

Rinse dried mushrooms and drain. Soak the dried mushrooms in ⅓ cup warm water for 30 minutes. Drain, reserving liquid. Chop mushrooms. Strain liquid through cheesecloth or very fine strainer. Set aside.

Heat butter and oil in a 3-quart saucepan. Cook onion and garlic in butter and oil until tender. Add chopped dried mushrooms; cook and stir for about 5 minutes. Add chopped fresh mushrooms and reserved liquid; cook and stir until almost dry.

Peel, seed and remove core from tomatoes; chop. Add tomatoes with seasonings and herbs to mushrooms; cook and stir about 5 minutes. Add broth; bring to a boil and simmer for 30 minutes to blend flavors. Check seasonings.

Serve with garlic toast, if desired.

MAKES 8 TO 10 SERVINGS.

PEPPERED ROAST

2 7-rib beef roasts	1 to 2 Tbsp. salt
(14 to 15 lbs.)	¼ cup cracked
1 or 2 large garlic cloves	black pepper

Have the butcher remove the chine bone, back cord and feather bone from roasts. Trim excess fat and bone ends.

Peel and mash garlic with salt to make a paste; spread it on all surfaces of the roast. Sprinkle with pepper, pressing it into the garlic paste until well covered.

Place roasts, bone side down, in large roasting pans. Roast in a large covered barbecue grill or in a 325° oven (may need 2 ovens). Roast until meat thermometer reads about 110° Remove roasts from oven. Pour off fat. Protecting hands with towels, stand both roasts up in one large pan with ribs facing each other. Cross every other rib to create a double rack roast.

Return double rack roast to oven, and roast 15 to 20 minutes per pound for medium rare. Roast until a meat thermometer reads 130° to 150° depending on desired doneness.

Let beef rest at least 15 minutes before carving. Serve with Oven Roasted Onions (see page 124), if desired.

MAKES 40 TO 50 SERVINGS.

Note: 4 or 5-rib roast may be used. Reduce seasonings by ⅓.

Brown Gravy: Remove roast to serving platter; keep warm. Pour off drippings; skim fat off meat juices, reserving ⅓ cup. Return reserved fat to roasting pan. Stir in ⅓ cup all-purpose flour. Add water to meat juices to make 2⅓ to 3 cups; pour into pan. Cook and stir until mixture boils and thickens. Season to taste.

REAL MINCEMEAT PIE WITH WHISKEY HARD SAUCE

1 cup chopped cooked beef
¼ lb. suet or cold butter, cut up
3 cooking apples, pared, cored and cut up
1 orange, cut up (seeds removed)
1 Tbsp. lemon juice

2 cups dried fruit (cherries, cranberries, raisins and/or currants)
¾ cup brown sugar
¼ tsp. salt
1 tsp. each, ground cinnamon and allspice

½ tsp. ground nutmeg
¼ tsp. ground cloves
⅛ tsp. ground ginger
1 cup apple or white grape juice
Pastry for double crust pie (see page 145)

Grind beef and suet together or chop in food processor. Chop apples and orange or add to processor, using an on and off motion. Combine all ingredients, except pastry, in a large cooking pot; simmer about 1 hour or until most of liquid is gone. Cool before continuing.

Prepare pastry as directed. Line a 9 or 10-inch pie pan with half the pastry; fill with cooled mincemeat. Roll out remaining pastry and position on top of filling; crimp edge and prick top. Bake in a 450° oven for 10 minutes; lower heat to 350° and bake for 30 minutes. Serve warm pie with Whiskey Hard Sauce.

Whiskey Hard Sauce: Beat together until smooth and light, 1 cup confectioners' sugar, 4 Tbsp. butter, 1 to 2 tsp. whiskey and a dash of salt. Refrigerate. Spoon on top of hot Mincemeat Pie.

THUMBPRINT COOKIES

1¼ cups all purpose flour
¼ tsp. salt
½ cup butter or margarine
½ cup brown sugar, packed

1 egg, separated
1 tsp. vanilla
¼ cup finely chopped semi-sweet chocolate

¼ cup finely crushed wheat cereal
¼ cup finely chopped almonds
⅓ cup jelly or preserves

Mix flour and salt together. Beat butter until soft; add sugar and beat until fluffy. Beat in egg yolk and vanilla. Stir in flour and chopped chocolate. Cover and chill.

Beat egg white slightly. Shape dough into 1-inch balls. Mix cereal and almonds. Dip dough balls in egg white and then into cereal nut mixture. Place on a greased cookie sheet. Press thumb into center of each cookie.

Bake in a 350° oven for 15 to 17 minutes. Cool. Fill thumbprint with jelly or preserves.
MAKES ABOUT 2½ DOZEN.

NUT BARS

½ cup unsalted butter or margarine
½ cup sugar
2 Tbsp. finely chopped candied orange peel
2 Tbsp. finely chopped candied citron or cherries
1 egg, whole
1 egg, separated
1½ cups all-purpose flour
¼ tsp. salt
¾ cup finely chopped pecans
⅓ cup chopped white or milk chocolate
1 tsp. water
1 to 3 Tbsp. colored sugar

Beat butter and sugar together until fluffy. Add candied fruit, whole egg and egg yolk; beat until well mixed. Combine flour, salt, finely chopped nuts and chocolate; add to first mixture, stirring to blend.

Shape into two 12-inch long loaves, about 2-inches wide and 1-inch high.

Lightly beat together the egg white and water, brush over loaves. Sprinkle with colored sugar.

Bake in a 350° oven for 25 minutes or until lightly browned. Lower oven temperatures to 325°.

Remove loaves from oven and cool 5 to 10 minutes. Cut diagonally into ¾-inch slices. Place cut side down on baking sheets and return to oven for 10 to 15 minutes or until lightly toasted.

MAKES ABOUT 3 DOZEN.

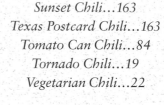

GLOSSARY

Definition of Terms

ALLSPICE

Available whole or ground, its strong, spicy flavor tastes like a combination of cinnamon, nutmeg and cloves. Used in desserts, meats and pickling.

BASIL

Sweet and pungent herb. Fresh leaves add a flavor to tomato-based dishes; dried, crushed leaves used in soups, sauces, with meats and fish.

BAY LEAVES

Adds a sweet, subtle flavor to meats, fish, soups and sauces. Since fresh leaves are often difficult to find, dried leaves are acceptable.

CARDAMOM

An aromatic spice used in baked goods, meat sauces and pickles. May be bought as dried pods containing small seeds, crushed or ground.

CILANTRO

A fresh, green herb resembling parsley in looks, but not taste. Sometimes called fresh coriander or Chinese parsley.

CLOVES

The dried flower buds of a tropical tree. Whole cloves add flavor to broth or soup stock; ground cloves often used in cookies and cakes at holiday time.

COLORED SUGAR

This may be purchased where cake and cookie decorations are sold. You can make your own by stirring a few drops of food coloring into the sugar.

COJACK

A cheese made by mixing colby, a mild yellow cheese, with Monterey Jack, a mild white cheese. Used in Tex-Mex cooking.

CORIANDER

Smells like sage and lemon peel, mixed. The small seeds are usually found ground; can be used in baking and desserts as well as in sausage and game cooking.

CORNMEAL

Ground dried white or yellow corn that is sometimes called masa.

CUMIN

Slightly bitter seeds; once used like pepper. They look like caraway seeds, and can be used the same way. May be added whole to sweet or spicy meat dishes, chili, dry beans or rice; also found ground.

CURRANTS

Dried, small seedless grapes. Chopped seedless raisins may be substituted.

DUTCH OVEN

Made of cast iron, they stand on short legs and have a slightly domed lid with a 2-inch rim around the edge. Bread bakers are 4-inches deep. Deeper ones are for meat. Preheat by standing it on the coals before adding food. Coals are placed on the lid so that food will brown and cook evenly from all sides. There are also Dutch Ovens that are made and sold for use in the kitchen. They look like the outdoor variety without legs. Follow the recipe and bake in a 350° to 400° oven or simmer on the top burner.

HOMINY

Dried corn that has been soaked in water and lime juice. Usually found in cans, it's sometimes called posole when found dried.

GLOSSARY

JICAMA

A root with juicy white flesh. It is crunchy and has a mild sweet taste, somewhat like a water chestnut. It can be eaten cooked as a vegetable or raw in salads and appetizers.

MACE

This ground spice is made from the lacey covering of the nutmeg. It is mild and fragrant, suggesting both nutmeg and cinnamon and works in sweets as well as in main dishes. Adds the final touch to dessert sauces such as Vanilla Custard or Whipped Cream.

MARGARITA SALT

A salt used to coat the rims of glasses; table salt may be substituted.

MARJORAM

A sweet, spicy herb, close to thyme in flavor. Dried or fresh, it's added to meat, fish, poultry, soups and stews.

MILLET

A food grain resembling a small pellet. Gives a good crunch and flavor to breads and cooked cereals.

OREGANO

A wild marjoram with a stronger flavor than sweet marjoram. Used in beef stews, tomato sauces, on grilled meat or fish; found dried or fresh.

PECTIN

A flavorless carbohydrate found in certain fruits that makes jams or jellies set and gel.

PEPPERS

Ancho. Dried Pablano peppers, almost black and wrinkled. Fresh, they resemble sweet peppers, but darker green, with a pointed end. A comfortable, but slightly hot taste.

Casabel. Small and round, with a smooth brownish-red skin; can be hot.

Caterina. Looks like the Casabel, but with a triangular shape; can be interchanged with it.

Chipotle. Ripe Jalapeños that have been dried and smoked. They are light brown, smell smoky, and are found canned in vinegar or in adobo sauce (chili powder, herbs and vinegar).

Finger Peppers. Slender red peppers about as long as a finger. Medium hot.

Guajillo. Long, slender and smooth-skinned, this dry pepper has a brownish-red skin and can be very hot.

Habanero. Plump, ruffled peppers. Very hot.

Jalapeño. Plump, with dark green skin. Both pepper and seeds are very hot. Also canned or pickled.

Pasilla. Long, slender, wrinkled and very dark. Very hot.

Serrano. Small, bright green, smooth skin. Pleasant but hot. Be careful of the seeds. Also available canned or pickled.

Glossary

PINE NUTS

Small, sweet nuts from the piñon pine tree that grows in the Southwest. In the fall, when the pine's cones open and the seeds fall to the ground, they're gathered and roasted.

ROSEMARY

A sweet-smelling shrub-like herb that can be used fresh or dried. Goes well with eggs, cheese, breads and biscuits; but more commonly used with meats and poultry.

SAGE

Broadleafed herb most often associated with turkey stuffing or pork sausage. Dried or freshly chopped, it can be sprinkled over roast pork, duckling–even biscuits.

SAVORY

Summer and winter savory have a similar, delicate and spicy flavor. A fresh or dried herb that's a good addition to meat, fish and poultry; also can be used to flavor eggs and soups.

SCALDED MILK

Milk that has been brought to the boiling point, but not boiled.

SUET

Beef fat. Used in making Christmas puddings and mincemeat pie. Sometimes used to lard less–tender meat cuts, such as rump.

THYME

There are many varieties of this small-leafed herb. Goes well with root vegetables, such as carrots or potatoes. Fresh or dried, it can be added to soups, stews and sauces. A good substitute for sage when cooking poultry.

TOMATILLOS

Related to the ground cherry or cape gooseberry. They have a papery husk that's removed before using. When ripe, they turn yellow, but are usually used while still green. They are not green tomatoes, and have their own distinctive taste.

WILD MUSHROOMS

These are more aromatic and flavorful than the common white mushroom cap. They can be bought dried or fresh in ethnic or gourmet groceries. The dried varieties are usually easier to find, and adding them to white mushrooms add a distinctive flavor. If fresh are unavailable use older domestic white mushrooms as they have more flavor than the tightly closed young ones.

***Porcinis** (Italian) **Cepes** (French). A brown-capped mushroom. They are 2-inches or larger in diameter.*

***Shiitakes.** Also called Forest or Oriental Black mushrooms. They resemble parasols and are similar in size to the above.*

***Chanterelles.** Shaped like flowers with frilled edges. They are very delicate and 2 to 3-inches in diameter.*

***Portobellos.** Resemble big brown parasols with black lining. They have a very firm texture and an almost meaty flavor.*

***Morels.** A popular springtime treat for wild mushroom hunters. They look like small spungy trees and have an unforgettable taste.*

***Oyster, Lobster** and **Enoke.** Other mushrooms, if available, that can be used.*

GLOSSARY

Special Methods

CANNING

Preparing Jars. Wash jars, rinse and sterilize in hot water before filling. Turn jar upside down to drain, but fill jars while they are still hot.

Filling Jars. Pour food mixture into hot jars, leaving some headroom. Jams and sauces need about ½-inch space between food and lid; pickles need about 1-inch. Use a jar filler—looks like a large-mouthed funnel—to pour foods, to keep jar edges clean for proper sealing.

Hot Water Bath. A method used for jams and pickles to prevent the formation of mold. Put filled and sealed jars onto a rack and lower in a deep kettle of boiling water. Water should be about 1-inch deeper than jars. Start counting when water starts boiling again; remove jars using a jar lifter when processing time is over. Cool on a rack.

CAST IRON CARE

Avoid washing cast iron pans, wipe them with paper towels instead. If food sticks, rinse in warm water with detergent and scour lightly with a brush or nylon pad. Dry well by heating over a burner or in a heated oven before putting away. When breaking in a new pan, follow directions from maker.

This usually means wiping with paper towels and heating over medium heat to remove any protective coating that may be on the pan. Wipe again before using. If washing is necessary, dry thoroughly as directed above.

COCOA PANCOAT

Combine 1 tsp. each, cocoa and flour with shortening to make a soft mixture. Use this to grease pans when baking chocolate cakes. Or, pans may be greased, then dusted with cocoa instead of flour.

COOKING MEAT

A meat thermometer is your best guide. Remember that internal temperature will rise after meat is taken from the oven, so remove roasts 5 to 10 degrees below the desired temperature.

COOKING WITH SPIRITS

Wine, whiskey and beer are added to meats and sauces for special flavor and tenderness. The alcohol is released during the cooking process. You can substitute broth, vegetable or fruit juice, or just water. Whatever you choose will give a different flavor to the end product.

PEPPERS (PREPARATION)

Hot Pepper Handling. Wear gloves when handling. Remove seeds and membranes before handling. Keep hands away from face until they've been carefully washed.

Roasting Sweet Peppers. Big red, green or sweet peppers are best when roasted and peeled before adding to salads and vegetable dishes. They can be roasted in a hot oven (450°) or broiled until brown and charred. Turn them often as they cook. When charred on all sides, place in a paper bag and let them cool—about 30 minutes. Strip peelings and discard. Also, discard seeds and membrane before adding to recipe.

How Many? When a recipe gives a variable amount, start with the lesser amount, tasting and adding as you go. Pepper "heat" tends to increase overnight, so if you're cooking ahead, wait to add more after reheating your recipe.

"Heat" Levels. Habañeros are the hottest. Jalapeños are next. Serranos seem mild in comparison. Finger, Pablano and Anaheim peppers can vary in hotness, sometimes tasting almost mild.

GLOSSARY

PIE CRUST PREPARATION

Keep It Cool. Work rapidly, using cold ingredients, for a flaky crust. Handle dough as little as possible.

Roll It Easy. Shape dough into a round ball, flatten into a thick cake, and place in the center of a lightly floured pastry cloth or other surface. Roll from the center not from side-to-side to form a true round of even thickness. When desired size has been reached, fold pie crust twice (into quarters) or roll and wrap it around the rolling pin to move it to the pie pan.

Shaping Edge. Trim dough about ½ to 1-inch bigger than the pie pan. For a single crust, turn edge under, pressing firmly to make a collar. Pinch and shape edge as desired. The bottom of a double pie crust is trimmed close to the pie pan once it is filled. The top crust is cut about 1-inch larger than the pie pan. This overhang is tucked under the edge of the bottom crust and pinched to seal. Make cuts to vent top crust.

Testing Doneness. Test custard or pumpkin pie by inserting a clean silver knife into filling, about 1-inch from the center of pie. Do not insert in dead center—you'll overcook the pie (the center continues to cook after the pie is taken from the oven).

PROCESSING

This must be done if you are preserving food for later use. It can be done in a hot water bath (see page 161) to stop mold and spoilage in canned pickles and jams.

SALT BAG

Fill a small square of cotton cloth with salt, pull up corners and tie securely. Dip in oil and wipe over pancake griddle or skillet to lightly coat it with oil.

SOURDOUGH STARTER

Soften 1 package active dry yeast in 1 quart lukewarm water in a large crock or bowl. Add 2 Tbsp. sugar and 4 cups all-purpose flour. Beat to mix. Cover with a towel and place in a warm place to sour for 2 to 4 days. After mixture has reached desired sourness, keep it in the refrigerator.

If starter is not used often, stir flour and water into it every 10 days to keep it fresh and active.

SUBSTITUTING HERBS

Dried Herbs For Fresh. Use ⅓ to ½ the measured amount of fresh herbs suggested in the recipe. Mild and readily available herbs, such as parsley and chives, may be used in place of other fresh herbs at any time.

Fresh Herbs For Dried. Double or triple the dry herb amount. Fresh herbs are milder and smoother in taste, so more is desirable.

TABASCO® is a registered trademark and service mark exclusively of McIlhenny Co., Avery Island, Louisiana 70513.

POSTCARD CHILI RECIPES

CHILI PIT CHILI

4   slices smoked bacon
2   lbs. lean pork,
    cut into cubes
1½ cups chopped onion
2   large cloves garlic,
    minced
1   Tbsp. chili powder
1   tsp. dried oregano
¼   tsp. ground cumin
1   quart chicken broth
2   14½-ounce cans
    hominy, drained
6   Ancho chilies
2   10-ounce cans corn
    kernels, drained

   In a large kettle, over
medium heat, fry bacon until
crisp; remove bacon. Pour off
all but 2 or 3 Tbsp. bacon fat;
add pork. Cook and stir until
brown. Add onion and garlic;
cook and stir until onion is
tender.
   Crumble bacon and add
with chili powder, oregano,
cumin, chicken broth and
drained hominy; bring to
a boil.
   Wash dried ancho chili
pods, remove stems and
seeds; cut up with kitchen
shears and add to pork
mixture.
   Simmer 2 or 3 hours until
flavors blend and mellow,
adding chicken broth or
water if needed. Add corn
and heat.
MAKES 8 TO 10 SERVINGS.

SUNSET CHILI

4   lbs. ground lean beef or turkey
2 or 3 Tbsp. vegetable oil
2   28-ounce cans whole tomatoes
    in juice, cut up
2   15-ounce cans tomato sauce
2   cups light beer or water
¾   cup Chili Seasoning
    Mix (see page 24)
2   28-ounce cans pinto
    beans, optional

In a large chili kettle, brown meat in oil, stirring occasionally. Add
tomatoes, tomato sauce, beer and seasoning mix. Bring to a boil;
cover and simmer for 45 minutes. Rinse beans; drain and add to chili
mixture. Cover and simmer 15 to 20 minutes.
                     15 TO 20 SERVINGS.

TEXAS POSTCARD CHILI

1   lb. lean ground beef
½   lb. fresh hot sausage
1   cup chopped onion
1   cup chopped green pepper
2   Tbsp. chili powder
1   tsp. each, salt, dried
    oregano and
    ground cumin
¼   tsp. garlic powder
3 to 4 cups tomato juice
1   16-ounce elbow macaroni

   Brown beef and sausage
in a large fry pan. Add onion,
green pepper, cook and stir
until tender. Add seasonings
and about 3 cups tomato juice.
Cover and simmer.
   Cook macaroni 5 minutes,
in boiling salt water, drain and
add to meat mixture.
   Simmer 10 to 15 minutes,
to finish cooking macaroni and
blend flavors. Add more tomato
juice if needed.
MAKES 8 TO 10 SERVINGS.

NO-NAME CHILI

¼   lb. suet, finely chopped or
    3 to 4 Tbsp. cooking oil
6   lbs. lean beef, cut into
    ½-inch cubes
1   cup chili powder
2   Tbsp. ground cumin
2   Tbsp. ground oregeno
1   Tbsp. salt
1 to 2 Tbsp. cayenne pepper
4   cloves garlic, minced
2   quarts beef broth
    and/or water
½   cup finely ground
    cornmeal
½   cup cold water

   If using suet, fry it in a
large chili kettle until crisp.
Add beef to hot fat, 1 pound
at a time; cook and stir until
browned. Remove and repeat
with remaining beef.
   When all meat is browned,
return it to the kettle. Add seasonings and beef broth. Cover
and simmer 1½-2 hours. Skim
fat, if needed.
   Combine cornmeal with
cold water and stir into chili.
Simmer 30 minutes, stirring
occasionally.
MAKES 10 TO 12 SERVINGS.

NOTES